TRAVEL
UNSCRIPTED

TRAVEL
UNSCRIPTED

MARK MURPHY

HIGHPOINT
EXECUTIVE PUBLISHING
www.highpointpubs.com

New York — Los Angeles

This edition published by Highpoint Executive Publishing.
For information, write to info@highpointpubs.com.

First Edition

ISBN: 978-0-9839432-2-8

Library of Congress Cataloging-in-Publication Data

Murphy, Mark

Travel Unscripted

Includes index.

Summary: "Nationally recognized travel expert and television correspondent Mark Murphy chronicles the dicey, humorous, sometimes bizarre and always entertaining experiences he encounters in far-flung locales when he's not on camera." – Provided by publisher.

ISBN: 978-0-9839432-2-8 (hardbound)

1.Travel 2. Travelogue

Library of Congress Control Number: 2011945586

Design by Sarah Clarehart
Cover photo by Nick Choo
Interior photos copyright Performance Media Group except where noted.

Manufactured in the United States of America
10   9   8   7   6   5   4   3   2   1

Dedication

This book is dedicated to the hard-working travel agents who script the adventures for millions of consumers eager to explore the world.

Acknowledgments

Like most entrepreneurs I started out with one vision of what we were to build only to see it morph into something completely different. That's what happened in the case of online video. We never set out to shoot video, it just kind of happened. Luckily, I had some key people I could turn to when we made that decision.

Nick Choo, my producer, is one of the people that made this book a reality. He didn't write anything, but he did provide the knowledge and knowhow that put us into the video production game. His expertise has grown and it shows from one shoot to the next. Even though Nick didn't write a single word for the book, he provided plenty of material, as you'll read about. Gene Kang works with Nick and usually runs the sound and the second camera. He started with us a few years ago, and with Nick's help, has grown into a core part of our production team. When we are shooting on the road it's these two guys who make the shots work.

A special thanks to my editor Michael Roney and his team at Highpoint Executive Publishing, including Sarah Clarehart,

Ron Marr, Michael Utvich, Stacia Friedman, Michael Welch and Pilar Wyman. They all helped to bring the ideas for this book to life.

The company I own, and the stories we've created along the way, wouldn't have been possible without the encouragement and support of the most important person in my life...my wife Karen. When I was hemming and hawing about whether to start a company or stay in my comfort zone she gave me a good solid push. She knew what I needed to do even more than I realized at that time. With a three-year-old and a five-year-old at home she looked at our house in Rye, New York and said, "Let's sell this place and move. You need to do this." And that was that.

The company was born. *Travel Unscripted* would arrive later.

Viewing the Videos in This Book

A picture tells a thousand words, and when it comes to a moving picture...well, the experience is even better. *Travel Unscripted* is enhanced by numerous videos that will provide a richer perspective on many of the book's stories. Videos are indicated directly on the pages where you see the well-known video "Play" icon superimposed on the image. You can view any or all of these videos regardless of whether you're reading the e-book or the print edition. Here's how:

E-Book: For all Apple and Nook Color or Nook Tablet devices, simply click on any image with the "Play" icon and the video will start playing. For other devices, including Kindle Fire users, go to http://travelunscriptedbook.com/media.html to view videos. Check that page for updates as more readers become video-enabled.

Print Book: You can view any and all of the videos by going to http://travelunscriptedbook.com/media.html. Once there, just click on the one you want to see.

Contents

Introduction

There I was in the heart of Taiwan, standing in the middle of a field wearing a fireman's uniform. I was encased in the typical thick rubber jacket and pants, along with a motorcycle helmet featuring a full facemask. I was sweating like a pig and the outfit weighed a ton, but maybe that was a good thing, as I was surrounded by hundreds of revelers who were gleefully aiming highly incendiary fireworks at me. They intended to launch them soon.

I was given a wet towel to wrap around my neck so those pesky little rockets wouldn't explode around the area between the helmet and the jacket, and an ambulance waited nearby. I had that sinking feeling that this wasn't the smartest thing I'd ever done.

Just how did I get into this insane situation?

Well, it's all part of my job. I've been to more than fifty countries and counting, producing videos that showcase the memorable charms of medieval towns, luxe resorts and expansive cruises. I've met some interesting people and visited some exotic places along the way. In these shoots I work without a script, and

1

indeed, in the course of my travels you might say that things sometimes go *waaay* off script. There's no doubt that I've had more than my share of hair-raising predicaments and downright scary food.

In the Beginning

This all started many years ago when I was looking for a job in advertising in New York City. I had spent almost two years with the Nynex Yellow Pages, as they were known back then, in the pre-Internet Stone Age. I covered clients in three different boroughs: Manhattan, Brooklyn and Staten Island. Most of the clients were small-business owners who relied on the yellow pages for their entire existence.

I called on everyone from locksmiths to doctors and auto-repair shops. Many of these meetings started out with a loud complaint because the rates almost always went up, in some cases by double-digit increases each and every year. The company knew they were the only game in town for many of these businesses and extracted as much as they could.

It was one heck of a learning experience for a young guy out of college as it taught me how to deal with difficult people and the world of advertising. Difficult people were what I remembered the most, but I learned quite a bit about advertising and have applied those lessons to the travel business.

One other tidbit I learned during those two years was that I wanted to do something other than sell ads in a directory. I was interested in content that would drive people to explore something like a magazine, where the advertisements themselves simply rode along to speak to the audience. After my first year of selling directory space I realized that the job was definitely not for me and started to look for other opportunities.

In 1991 I ended up selling ads for a trade magazine called *Travel Agent*, and my timing couldn't have been better. I began that job just a few weeks before we started to bomb Baghdad in Operation Desert Storm. The business ground to a halt that year, but I was too new or wet behind the ears to really grasp it. I simply went out and focused on learning the space and the industry as a whole.

The guy who hired me was someone named John Ballantyne, a Harvard grad who immediately reminded me of the actor James Cagney. He was small, but you wouldn't mess with him even if you weighed quite a bit more. He just had this edge about him that told you he'd just as soon knock you on your ass as look at you. He was also the guy you'd want in the foxhole with you when you went to war. John is best described simply as a guy's guy.

John's favorite word was "fuck." I heard a lot of it during my first and only interview for the job. I sat in his office while he explained the history of both himself and his boss, Richard Friese. The two of them were running the business with Friese as the publisher and John as the associate publisher.

As the interview got underway John said, "So I was coaching Friese's kid and he told me I should get out of this coaching and come work for him." Friese was the head of something called Hotel and Travel Index at the time and thought John could do much more in the business world than as a teacher at some private school, as was his current career. He'd certainly make more money, but more importantly, he would be in an environment that better matched his style. I don't know about you, but academia hardly seemed like a good fit for John, hearing him speak. "Friese fucking ran *Travel Weekly* and made it number one and now we're going to do the same thing for fucking *Travel Agent* magazine."

I didn't know anything about travel or the media business at that time, but I did know that I liked to go out there and mix it up competitively. In fact, I hate to lose.

I was the sixth kid in a family of seven, so I'm pretty sure my fighting spirit was always necessary for self-preservation. I had to fight for attention because my parents got to the point where they simply lost track of me. I remember the day when my mom headed home from a day of shopping and simply forgot one of us. Fortunately for me it was my little brother Mike. Nothing happened to Mike, but imagine if that happened today. She'd be arrested and charged with child neglect.

I sat there and took in John's stories about his days with Friese, the competitive nature of the business, and their success. I knew I wanted to be part of this team and what would be a turnaround situation. The magazine I was about to join had fallen on some hard times, so I knew any turnaround was going to be tough work. It was very clear that this team would be focused on replicating the same success that had occurred earlier with *Travel Weekly*, albeit with a unique approach to the market.

It was a strange interview because all I did was sit there with my mouth shut. Most interviews in my life have consisted of being asked a bunch of questions that have you sharing your experiences or accomplishments with an eye on impressing the interviewer. In this case it was as if John was selling me on the job instead of the other way around.

It was nice not to have to deal with all of those stupid questions that are so typical of a sales interview. If you've ever been through one then you know what I'm talking about. How great would it be to have it go like the following, instead of how it typically has to go? That is, if you actually are trying to get fired before you get hired!

4

Interviewer: "Tell me about one thing you are most proud of and what that meant to you at the time."

Answer: "The fact that I stayed out till 3:00 a.m. and still made it to my 8:00 a.m. meeting without throwing up on my shoes?"

Interviewer: "What motivates you?"

Answer: "Taking your job in a year when it becomes clear that I work harder and smarter than you do..."

Interviewer: "What would your coworkers say about you?"

Answer: "That I'd sell my mother to make a deal?"

Interviewer: "Give an example of when you had to change your approach to a prospect because the initial one failed."

Answer: "I actually had to go on a sales call instead of waiting for someone to send me an order via my telepathic Vulcan mind meld."

Interviewer: "Where do you see yourself in five years?"

Answer: "Running this place with you as my bitch?"

Interviewer: "Tell me about your views when it comes to working with a team?"

Answer: "There is no I in T-E-A-M but there sure as fuck are an M and an E."

Interviewer: "Why did you apply for this position?"

Answer: "There wasn't anything else available."

If only once you could have this kind of fun on an interview! Imagine the look on the interviewer's face, especially if your first interview is with someone from the human resources department. Priceless!

That wasn't going to happen on my interview with John because he didn't bother to ask me a single question during the one-hour I sat in his office. Indeed, I barely said a word the entire time. What he did do was to emphasize every statement he made with "fuck" or "fucking." At the end of an hour he asked if I had any questions. He had told me virtually everything possible about the company and the position, so I replied with "When do you want to make me an offer?" I was offered the job the following day and quickly took John up on it.

The Power Play

I was excited about the idea of a fresh start, as my previous job had become a real bore. The competitive landscape also fueled that spirit I had always felt in my days as an athlete. The challenges that were laid out in the interview made me excited to be part of this new team.

Unfortunately, things got off to a bit of a slow start as I was the new guy and was handed the "scraps"—all the accounts that nobody else wanted to handle. To give you an idea of these accounts and their stature, look no further than the Tipton County Pork Festival, an Indiana-based event that had done some advertising with us in years past and was one of my initial clients. I recall that they spent about $2,000 per year on small space ads that ran in a special supplement we produced quarterly. The likes of Pan Am, Eastern Airlines and TWA were all big advertisers back then and had been shielded from my territory by other sales people, at least in the early days.

After a couple of weeks on the job I realized that I wasn't going to be challenged at all. I had about forty accounts and they mostly resembled Tipton County in stature. It doesn't take too much time to contact that number of accounts, understand their needs, and then move on. For me it was roughly two weeks. As a Type A personality, I couldn't simply sit around and collect a paycheck, so I took it upon myself to approach John with my concerns and thoughts on this new position. To sum it up, I told him that I didn't accept the job just so I could sit around and do nothing. I told him that I didn't have enough accounts and if this was how it was going to be, I'd be better off going somewhere else. Ballantyne reacted by telling me, "I'll take care of it, just be patient. Give me a couple of weeks." (I'm pretty sure it was punctuated by a couple of fucks along with his trademark laugh.)

I agreed to sit tight and had barely made it back to my desk when he called out to all the sales staff and we assembled at his desk. John's first attempt to get things evened out on the account front took place at that point. He told us to go in a room and "divide up accounts." If you understand anything about sales, it's that revenue matters. Indeed, that's how you get paid. Give away an account that's running business with you and you get paid less. So, needless to say, this little exercise turned out to be a waste of time.

After that debacle I marched into John's office and told him that this just wasn't going to work for several reasons. Again he told me to be patient and he'd "fix it." I wandered out of his office wondering what the heck "fixing it" would mean. It didn't take more than a few minutes to find out.

I heard him almost immediately call out for Nancy Ness. Nancy was a salesperson who had been with the magazine for several years at that point. She was part of the team that John inherited when he was brought in to run the day-to-day operations of the business. Nancy was great to me when I started as she was open and tried to help me acclimate to the company while the others simply went about their business. She was incredibly helpful in showing me what needed to be done as part of my day-to-day job. That's why what came next was so difficult to watch.

When Nancy made it to his office and sat down, I had no idea what was going to take place. It took all of about one minute and she was walking out of John's office visibly shaken. Her eyes had misted up, but before I could even ask her what was up John yelled out for me, "Hey Murphy, get in here."

I went to his office and he told me that he had taken care of my problem. He had just fired Nancy and was giving me her territory. Oh boy, I thought. No wonder she's upset! He said, "Look, she's a little upset right now, so don't bother her yet, but you'll need to sit down with her and review the accounts. She's staying on for a few weeks so you'll be able to do it next week. Just give her a little bit of time."

I left John's office and went back to my station. I gave Nancy a sincere sorry and she said thanks. I then turned my attention to my desk as I didn't know what else to say. I stayed that way for a few minutes, not sure what to do next. It was Tuesday and I had absolutely nothing to do the remainder of the week. I had already reached out to all of my existing clients and prospects and had even read the latest issue of the magazine. Being incredibly impatient I was only able to remain quiet for so long. I was jumping at the chance for some new challenges as I turned toward Nancy and blurted out "Want to review the accounts...?"

Bad move. If looks could kill, I would have been dead at that moment. The time between that announcement and her firing was somewhere less than ten minutes. I'd learn to be a little more sensitive in future situations, but this time I really blew it.

The transition did take place, with Nancy being a great help to me. She moved on and eventually went to work for another publishing company in New York City. As of this writing, almost twenty years after that fateful day, she's still at her new company and thriving.

New Beginnings

John didn't have any use for the president of the company at the time and used his colorful approach to language in an ongoing battle with him. He felt like he reported to Friese and that was that. On more than one occasion I would stare in amazement as I sat in his office and he would answer the phone…the call coming from the company president. A moment after answering it I'd hear him say, "Bruce, go fuck yourself!" It was definitely funny to witness, as you couldn't believe that he was actually saying it, and more important, getting away with it.

However, it eventually caught up to him and John was moved to the company's new digital publishing group. The company had no such division, so it was basically a way for John to finish out his time and search for another position.

I enjoyed many of John's crazy antics and really enjoyed working with him, but the real value of my time with him and Friese came down to their approach to the business. I've taken many of the lessons I learned in those early years and have applied them to my business today and can credit a lot of my success to those experiences. These lessons directly influenced the formation of our *Travel Unscripted* video productions.

Travel Unscripted was started based on the belief that you had to have a unique position in a large market. Travel agents accounted for more than one hundred billion dollars in travel sales so they certainly qualified as a large market. The approach to building a business in this massive space was simple. Look at how the media category was currently serving travel agents and address the most glaring gaps.

For instance, at the time, most magazines printed seven-day-old news and thought that was good enough. This presented an opportunity to address the agent's information needs leading to the real-time news service that became TravelPulse.com.

Problem was, our business was launched within six months of the 9/11 attacks. At that time, launching a media business focused on travel seemed downright silly. People weren't traveling and the main audience for this new business was travel agents. Hey…Murphy's law strikes again!

Fortunately, we were being built as a dot com with a lower cost structure than our competitive set, but our future really came down to three questions: The travel business—would it continue to grow? Innovation—could we bring it? Travel agents—would consumers continue to use them, at least to some degree?

As everyone knows in hindsight, the travel business came roaring back and saw tremendous growth throughout most of the past decade. The media industry, meanwhile, saw tremendous disruption. Both trends helped us to build a unique and sustainable business driven by innovation and being ahead of the market. Much of this success was tied to our ability to see trends, and more importantly to make the right investments and get ahead of the trends.

We did this back in 2005 when video on the web was struggling and most people weren't even able to watch streaming video due to bandwidth issues. That didn't stop us from seeing the potential, especially when it came to travel—we understood that bandwidth would grow to accommodate this new medium. So we spent tens of thousands of dollars on equipment to get into the online video world. I didn't worry about making money or even what would happen in the near term. My only thought was to get into the space because that's where media was moving. That move wouldn't take place, though, until a key person joined our team based on absolutely nothing to do with video.

The Choo Breakthrough

Early that same year I interviewed a young college kid named Nick Choo for a marketing position in our company. He had an undergraduate degree from Emerson College in Boston and a Master's degree from Florida State. I didn't pay much attention to his résumé or his degrees, only his website and examples of his work. That to me was the key, and is *the* key, to hiring most people—what they are capable of doing, not what school or specific classes they took.

He was applying for a marketing job, but he just didn't seem like a "marketing guy." I just couldn't imagine him doing marketing based on our conversations and his body of work, or his head, for that matter. Nick's hair was bleached a bright shade of white, something not entirely common among Asians. He seemed destined for more creative endeavors. A buttoned-up marketing position was definitely not going to cut it in his case. It made me take a pass on Nick and I ended up hiring another person in that position.

What I didn't know at the time was that Nick had a student visa and it was about to run out. He had to find employment to stay in

The Terminator? No, just Nick with his Steadicam.

the country and that employer would have to sponsor him for an H-1B work visa. A few weeks before he was scheduled to leave the country I reached out to Nick on a whim. I had a website that needed to be built and thought he'd be able to do it based on what he had done for his own personal site. I tried to get him to take it on as a project until he said he couldn't because he needed full-time employment status in order to stay in the United States. Even though I didn't have an actual job, just a project, I went ahead and hired him. When he asked what he was going to be doing I explained the website project that needed to be completed and the timeframe to get it done. His next question was, "What happens after that"? My answer was immediate: "I have no idea, but I'm sure we'll figure out something."

Little did I know at the time that taking a risk on this new employee would help us immensely in future years as we developed Travel Unscripted, the concept behind our videos and our approach to shooting them on location all over the world.

The idea for shooting video was based on a simple premise, that online video would be the future of the media industry. As broadband penetration increased, we figured that more and more people would have access to, and consume, video content. The fact that you can actually share a video online versus one that is on broadcast or cable networks made for an even better situation. Everyone today talks about "viral" marketing, but back then it was barely in anyone's vocabulary. That was sure to change.

One other detail helped to seal the deal. When you look at the travel space it's interesting to contrast the written word with the visual aspects of video. If you could bring a resort or destination to life on video you would have a powerful tool to drive demand. These factors drove our early investments in the space, which have continued as we constantly try to push the envelope and challenge ourselves to create better content.

So a couple of months before most people heard of YouTube, we started working on a concept to put a unique video on our main website, TravelPulse.com, each and every day. As we sat around discussing how we might be able to do this, with me fully caffein-ated and jumping out of my seat, as is typical, Nick was noticeably silent. As I've learned over the years, this is pretty typical of his personality. We were pretty far along in the conversation when he finally piped up and said he thought he could help. He then explained how his communications degree was actually in *film* and he had studied film both in college and in grad school. He explained what we would need to get started and some other insights. It was like, *duh, when were you going to tell us this!?*

Baby Chick Dave

A few weeks later we were loaded up with the latest equip-ment and ready to begin our daily show. The idea was to start with a news report summarizing some of the latest news in the industry. One of our early partners, David Lovely, took the role of anchor. His first segments were produced in a hotel room while we were at a travel convention in Montreal. Dave was sitting at the desk, and as I recall, he was in his underwear with a button-down shirt and tie. It was an interesting combination.

Our initial videos were shot with a professional Canon camera, but had no set design to make our production look better. It was Dave sitting in an office with his new "hairstyle." The hairstyle was a direct result of a bad decision to bleach his hair. Even though the woman who cut his hair warned him against doing this, Dave went ahead anyway. He didn't have a lot of hair to begin with and he didn't mind damaging what was left in the process. Although he didn't really destroy his hair, he did earn the nickname "Baby

Baby Chick Dave was not wearing pants.

Chick" when the results were clear. That moniker came from the woman who actually did the treatment and almost suffered a heart attack from laughing when she saw the result.

One of the things you might notice from the picture is how Dave's head would glow in the overhead fluorescent lights of our office. We used an extra office as our regular 'set' and taped cue cards to the wall for Dave to follow. He did his best to report in an authoritative way, but his scruffy beard, white hair and reflecting forehead competed for attention with the news, at least to me. It didn't stop Dave or our team from fulfilling on the commitment to shoot, edit and deliver a new episode each day of the business week. We were committed to the cause and used these early exercises to get acclimated to turning out some content, even if it was less than exciting (sorry, Dave).

Getting Creative

Shooting creative videos on location didn't always go smoothly, as we quickly discovered. We had to work hard to come up with content that would be interesting to watch, unbiased, and informed. This was no easy task given how varied many of these shoots were. We put together most trips on the fly, with little time to prepare in advance or to properly research what we would be covering. We were innovative in our approach, as we had no other choice. Indeed, the saying "necessity breeds innovation" pretty much sums up how we made things work.

In the early years Sandals Resorts hired us to film all seventeen of their properties. They would feature me, as the host, showcasing each resort while interviewing staff and, if possible, guests. That included interviews where the general manager or another staff member could share his or her thoughts on what made the property unique.

Although this coverage was effective to some degree, something was missing. It was effective because it took the concept of a virtual property tour to a new level by providing perspective while you watched. It added the element of an on-camera narrative, but it missed the experience of the stay or the journey that brought you to a particular place, regardless of whether it was a hotel or even a restaurant. That's what we thought was missing from the videos we were shooting as we continued to look for ways to improve the process and the final output.

Because we almost always work with a busy travel company or a destination property as part of our video productions, we run into situations that have led us to our approach: travel unscripted. With plenty of other demands on their time these organizations do their best to help us get the logistics together, but it almost always comes down to winging things at the last minute.

During a trip to Taiwan, described later in this book, we realized that we can't be part of a conventional media trip or what is known as a *familiarization trip* if we are to be successful in our efforts to produce good content. Given a choice between shooting yourself—this is, with a gun—or going on one of these trips and trying to produce video, you might choose the first. It would be less painful so long as it wasn't fatal.

A familiarization trip is designed for travel agents or meeting planners to experience a particular product like a hotel or a destination. It's an organized affair where the days are chock full of "inspections" that have you racing from one location to another with the goal of covering as much ground as possible. These are the last things you want to be diddling with when trying to shoot video, because you never have a chance to shoot a thing of substance. There just isn't any time for it. On the other hand a media trip is a little less jammed, but still takes the concept of more is better to heart. On these trips, the vast majority of participants are travel writers. They observe, take notes, and ultimately write stories about their experience. That story might get written that night, on the flight home or a month after the experience.

You can't do that with video. If you are there to shoot video you either get it done or you don't. You can do some post production work such as transitions and voice-overs, but you need the baseline content to work with. That's why we always turn down media tours that other reporters or writers are attending. We send our writers there, but leave our cameras and sound equipment at home. We go only when we are free to roam and capture what we need to capture. Schedules won't be tolerated, but that's not how it always was.

It was on a trip to Taiwan where we discovered how we had to operate if we were going to elevate our game and create some really great videos that could go up against the stuff you see on the Travel Channel and other outlets. I'll talk more about it later in the book, but suffice it to say, Taiwan was the launching pad for doing things differently. We were part of a group on that trip and had to break away each time we wanted to accomplish anything worth producing, unless filming senior citizens eating porridge was part of the script. We eventually left the group and ended up creating the best content we had produced up until that time. Travel Unscripted was officially born.

1

Asleep in Vegas

What happens in Las Vegas, stays in Las Vegas. That advertising campaign has been key to the resurgence of the destination and the adult playground it truly is. The dude I discovered curled up in my hotel hallway could probably have attested to the wisdom of Sin City's ridiculously successful slogan if only he had been able to regain consciousness while I was around.

But I'm getting ahead of myself.

If you recall, Vegas tried to reposition itself for the family market many years ago with little success. At the time it seemed like a sound strategy, so the hotel industry added roller coasters, aquariums and battling pirates. Families did indeed come, but unfortunately they didn't bring the gaming revenues that make the billion-dollar investments in the destination so profitable.

Maybe if they came in bigger numbers or spent more money in the casinos the strategy could have stuck. Then again, maybe not. I don't know about you, but I find it difficult to think about dragging my kids around Las Vegas when the street corners are

Family travel? It depends on your definition of "family."

covered with those small cards promising naked girls delivered to your room in twenty minutes. That's not a great message for a teenage boy or a young girl, and I have both. My son would certainly enjoy the pictures of the girls, but that's not something I'm ready to deal with at this point.

Reverting to Form, Vegas Style

As you can see, Vegas has a sex appeal that is far from discreet, and you don't have to see the sex trade itself to understand. Go into any casino and the cocktail waitresses are stuffed into tiny, revealing outfits as they work the tables in high heels, slinging drinks and cigarettes. You'll even see pole dancing in what's known as the Passion Pit when you venture into Planet Hollywood. Here, dancers will strut their stuff in lingerie, including g-strings, as gamblers below them place their bets. Distracting? You bet, but maybe that's the idea! What it all adds up to is an "adult paradise" that lets you take a walk on the wild side—if only for a few days.

If you really want to bring out your wild side you can take advantage of the fact that booze is flowing everywhere. That decision may lead to an Excedrin moment, as many individuals I came across were on their way to experiencing. I saw far too many future victims walking around with plastic booze guitars, filled with 100 ounces of their favorite alcoholic intoxicant with straws sticking out of the tops. Classy. I wonder what Frank or Sammy would have to say about that?

Some others with similar motivations had what looked like a huge water pipe, or bong, hanging from a strap around their necks. The theory behind the strap is to provide additional support for the weighty booze that's encased in the pseudo-bong. Let's face it, their arms couldn't support that kind of weight for too long as they made their way, along with their guitar heroes, to complete annihilation by 6:00 p.m. (Well, at least the booze bongs have a somewhat practical design.)

Have no fear, though, as passing out at 6:00 p.m. doesn't have to ruin the day or evening. A few hours later these same people will seemingly rise from the dead just in time for the club scene to kick into full gear. Let the party continue!

Now at this point you might understand why I leave my kids home when I come to town. When I'm home I can be the responsible dad and keep everything in check and my kids on their toes. When I come here I can people-watch or join the fray and cut loose. You never rent a car in Las Vegas so you never have to worry about having to drive or anything other than having a good time. By visiting without the kids, I'm not burdened with having to explain all the things that happen here to my very curious offspring.

If you have never been here on a holiday you can take it from me: Las Vegas has a way of putting you into a veritable time warp. Time seems to take on a different dimension, as does the sky. Indeed, as the day changes, so does the lighting on the sky-painted ceilings in both the Forum Shops at Caesars as well as the Canal Shops at the Venetian. It's very subtle, but you'll notice it if you pay attention. That's about the only indoor clue you'll get to what the real time is.

My suggestion: Forget about the actual time and just focus on the entertainment opportunities at hand. You may go all night and not realize it until you walk outside and see the sun coming up in the distance, being fooled for a moment into thinking it's sunset. Sorry friend, but you are back in the time warp!

So what did Las Vegas do a few years ago? It decided to reposition itself again for what it really is, an adult playground, by launching one of the most successful advertising campaigns in history. The campaign revolves around the saying, "What happens in Vegas, stays in Vegas," and is now used to describe any number of things we all do as adults that we don't want anyone else to know about.

Have you ever used this saying? I'll bet you have, and sometimes you actually meant it. You might have been up to no good and needed to avoid asking for a "get out of jail free card." The whole idea is to avoid jail in the first place by keeping what happens in some other dimension locked up right where it took place. That's my take at least.

Morning Weirdness

So what brings me to this glittering city? Most of the time when I come here I'm booked for meetings, a conference, or a TV appearance on one of the local affiliates for ABC, CBS or another network. That makes getting out and having a good time a little more challenging as I have to be game on for whatever it is I have to do. Most of the local morning shows run from 6:00 to 7:00 a.m. ahead of the nationally syndicated shows such as *Today* or *Good Morning America*. They cover local news, weather, traffic and lifestyle segments in that hour. When I get a chance to speak on one of these stations it's typically to talk about places I've been to or places that locals can visit in the months ahead. It's part travel trends, part travel tips and plenty of ideas based on places I've been and things I've done.

On this particular trip my publicist had me scheduled to appear at 6:20 a.m. on the CBS affiliate's Saturday-morning program. These local stations typically don't have someone on staff to do hair and makeup for guests or for their anchors, so everyone fends for himself or herself. That means you need to arrive "camera ready," which I did on that particular morning. There was a little problem. There was no show on Saturday. My publicist had given me the wrong day!

I didn't know this as I rolled out of bed at the crack of 4:45 to get ready. I took a shower and threw on the makeup that's necessary given the glaring lights and high-definition broadcasts that are the norm these days. I took a look in the mirror, gave myself the thumbs up and headed for the door.

As I stepped out into the hall I looked up and saw a body lying in the middle of it. It was clearly a man and he was curled up on his side and snoring heavily about forty feet away. This guy had decided that this would be his final resting spot after a night of partying. Who knows how long he had been there. He definitely was not waking up.

I gently nudged him and all I could get out of him was a grunt and another snore. This guy was out. When someone chooses to literally stop, drop and make a hotel corridor one's bedroom for the evening, that person is beyond salvage. That's what this guy seemingly did.

So here's what I did. I pulled out my iPhone and decided to capture this moment to share with my buddies. It's not too often you get to see a guy sleeping in the middle of a hotel hallway curled up in the fetal position. I took a couple of quick shots, shook my head, and then went back to trying to wake him.

After a few more nudges along with corresponding grunts from this Victim of Vegas, I ran out of time and needed to get going or I'd miss my appearance.

I had to head for the studio so I figured I'd tell the front desk about this guy who had taken a major broadside hit, and then I'd grab a taxi. Well, I was so focused on figuring out where Channel

"Help! I've fallen and I can't get up!"

8 Drive was located, and how long it might take me to get there, that I completely forgot about the poor sucker.

His comically disturbing visage popped back into my mind just as I was standing outside a very dark building at 5:45 on a Saturday morning. "Oh man…whoops!" Well, someone must have stumbled across him by now, or so I thought, so he should be good.

As I stood outside the studio, tapping my feet and dialing the phone extensions that would put me in touch with the producer, I still hadn't figured out that there was nothing going on this particular day. These early morning shows are a bit on the quiet side and you typically go around to a side door that they tell you about and knock on—or, as in the case here, ring an extension from an outside phone to have someone come and get you. It's not like the receptionist is sitting there at 6:00 a.m.! I wasn't surprised when someone didn't immediately pick up. I grew more concerned as the minutes passed and I might risk missing my slot.

Finally, after about fifteen minutes of trying, and feeling a bit stressed, I noticed some movement through the glass in the lobby. A small old man was making his way, very cautiously, toward me. He looked as if he was approaching a wild animal and seemed a bit stressed himself. He must have been thinking, "Who the hell is this person ringing these extensions?" I called each and every one and wasn't shy about letting them ring. I'm guessing he got so annoyed at hearing the phone ring and ring that he finally got up to see what's what. When he came across me he had that confused dog look. You know the one where they cock their heads back and forth as if trying to understand what you are saying.

He finally got the fact that I was there for an interview and then quickly told me there was no show that day. As I absorbed that fact I turned around and looked at my surroundings. The sun had yet to make its appearance and I could see nothing except a couple of shopping strips there at the north end of Las Vegas Boulevard. I told the old man thanks and walked from the studio building toward the cross street with the hope of grabbing a taxi back to my hotel.

Instead of a taxi approaching I saw a number of what I would describe as "characters" who seemed to be ready for bed, not the start of their day. I stood out like a sore thumb in my suit and made up face and noticed a couple of them casting some strange glances in my direction. I quickly turned left and headed toward Las Vegas Boulevard and to the Encore hotel, a short walk away. I would be able to catch a taxi there and get back to my hotel for some sleep.

This Stays in Vegas

While all this was going on the guy on the floor had vaporized from my thoughts, but it all came back to me in a rush when I stepped off the elevator and turned toward my room. There he was again, this time in a slightly different position. *Jesus Christ* I thought. He's still here! I tried to rouse him once again and this time he was even less responsive. I headed back to the elevator, saw the house phone, and called the operator. A few minutes later a security guy stepped off the elevator and we walked down the hall toward the guy on the ground.

At this point I noticed Sleeping Beauty's wallet lying next to him, so I handed it to the guard—but not until after I noted the guy's name and address on his driver's license. Nobody had tried to take any of his money or his identification, as everything still seemed to be intact. I gave the guard my estimate of how long the dude might have been laying here.

"I don't think you're going to be able to move him on your own. He's a pretty big guy," I added.

"I think we'll be able to get him up," the guard replied.

I suggested that he might want to call another one of his colleagues.

"Isn't he your friend?" the guard asked.

"I have no idea who he is, but you can check his name against the guest list to see if he's staying in the hotel or not."

I wished the guard luck, and headed off to my room to catch up on some sleep. I figured that the floor guy was now safe and that I had done my good deed, at least for that day. I slept for a couple of hours and awoke to a late-morning sun and went downstairs to grab a cup of coffee and something to eat at the Starbucks located in the casino.

I had brought my iPad and settled in to read a bit and enjoy some time of my own for a change. I contrasted how I was feeling at the moment, which was pretty good, to how the guy on the floor might be feeling at that same moment. I thought it might be funny, in a sadistic way, to ask him!

With more than 800 million people on Facebook, I figured that the guy on the floor was probably on it. I signed into my account and searched his name and hometown and found someone who seemed to match. It was tough to tell from his distorted features on the ground, but I thought it was likely. I sent him this message: "Robert, I think I just saw you in Las Vegas! What are you up to?" If it was the right guy he might have responded with "Getting my stomach pumped out" or "getting my diaper changed from last night."

However, the guy I pinged never responded so I'll never really know if he and the sleeper were one and the same. Still, I'll bet if I ever did meet him, he would describe the worst hangover he's ever had in his life, and maybe, just maybe, the sordid tale behind it. It would be the kind of story he would tell only to me—certainly not to his girlfriend or boss or—heaven forbid— his wife. It seemed pretty clear to me that this particular experience would "stay in Vegas."

2

River Cruising Unscripted

Back in the 90s Bill Clinton wagged his finger at the camera and sternly proclaimed "I did not have sexual relations with that woman." No one really believed him. When it came to pursuit of the opposite sex Bill was more wound up than an Arkansas razorback in springtime—but most people were more amused than appalled.

That's pretty much how I feel about Nick Choo. Nick denies that he's a smoker, and I deny that he's not. It's a silly charade—his clothes give off the distinctive aroma of a tour guide at a cigarette factory and in no way do I believe he wears Marlboro-scented aftershave—but it's a shtick we play out time and time again.

I don't really mind that Nick smokes; I just wish he'd come up with more inventive lies. Bill Clinton taught us that a little bravado goes a long way. If Nick would pull out a fake prescription pad and claim his doctor told him he was low on tar and nicotine I'd let the matter drop. I'd have been barely bothered by the fact that he was wrecking my schedule, wheezing, gasping and trailing far behind

"I'll never smoke again…"

on our uphill trek to Reichsburg Castle in Koblenz, Germany.

Nick staggered along, trying my patience and sucking more air than a Cat 5 hurricane on a gin jag. I wondered why I, at the age of forty-seven, was waiting on this thirty-year-old kid who appeared sorely in need of an industrial-strength respirator. This wasn't even a mountain we were traversing. We were walking up a nice, steady incline in the hopes of getting some good shots of the village, the river and our riverboat below.

I wondered if we would ever get there. Nick was bent over with his head between his knees, making a noise that reminded me of a water buffalo with the bends. He seemed to be wondering why this trip didn't involve helpful Sherpas with a mobile oxygen bar. I was about to pull out my iPhone, call up New York Presbyterian Hospital and inquire about the estimated wait time for prospective lung transplant recipients. At the rate we were traveling, a couple of barely used lungs might be available for delivery before we made it to the top of the hill.

Then it hit me that there was a much cheaper solution to the problem. We just needed more equipment. In addition to all the camera gear we typically haul around, we required motorized transport. We needed a Nickmobile or, more aptly named, a "Choo Choo." We could modify a Hoveround or a Rascal scooter, or perhaps wangle a deal on one of those electric carts Walmart provides for the severely obese Twinkie shopper. Those karts seem to have an infinite load limit, the perfect device for hauling our entire supply of lenses, tripods and lights.

As I waited for Nick to catch up (he was crawling on all fours by this point), I smiled at the wonders of modern science. Next time I would just strap our resident nicotine fiend to a custom

Choo Choo. I could maneuver him through tiny alleys in third-world backwaters, through the rubble-strewn plazas of Aztec ruins. Attach a remote steering device and I'd be in total control.

I smiled again as Nick finally reached my position. He'll never know how close he came to being deemed technologically redundant. Unless, of course, he reads this book.

Lazy Boy Cruising

Photo opportunities and emphysema aside, these riverboat cruises are not known for excitement or surprises. This is especially true when traveling with a small crew whose communication skills consist of dead silence or lung-rattling coughs. The mellow atmosphere is further enhanced by the fact that the average age of the other cruisers is generally around sixty-five. Sunbathing, kickboxing and limbo contests are out. Leisurely strolls, an early dinner and on-call electrocardiograms are in.

This is by design rather than coincidence. River cruises in Europe cater to an older demographic; they're really not intended for younger couples or families. The target market is usually upper-income couples age sixty or older, folks who prefer an endless seafood buffet and a nice view over a sensible fruit plate and an afternoon of mountain biking. The river cruise is basically the La-Z-Boy recliner of excursions. It's comfortable, it's relaxing and nobody is going to be shocked or surprised if you nod off for a few hours.

I'm a fair bit younger than the typical river-cruise client. I've not even begun to consider custom-fitted walkers, a hip replacement or adult undergarments, Still, there's at least one aspect of the experience that could lead me to consider river cruising as my full-time mode of transport.

River cruising provides "see" days.

It involves my socks.

The worst thing about traveling to far-flung countries is the constant packing and unpacking. Navigating the nooks and crannies of any given locale—no matter if it's southeast Asia or southwest Arizona—requires a great deal of movement. A great deal of movement translates to a great number of hotels. When I'm aboard a ship I unpack only once. My socks, shirts and underwear go from suitcase to dresser drawer in one fell swoop. That's where they stay. The ship is home base, the comforting spot to which you return after disembarking to take in a castle, cave, historic monument or local folk legend who carves Buddha figurines from panda dung and coconut husks.

This is not the case when we're journeying by car, foot, donkey or Camel Lights. It seems a good chunk of my time is wasted with checking in and checking out of hotels, loading and unloading suitcases, trunks and backpacks. I'd hire an official packer if one were available. Unfortunately, none of the people uniquely qualified for this position are willing to leave Green Bay.

The downside of river cruising is the slow pace and the tendency of some cruisers to endlessly discuss their favorite episode of Matlock. The upside is well-anchored bedroom furniture without the issue of getting seasick, as well as incredible scenery and access to small villages and local culture.

However, this trip was turning into something a little out of the ordinary. The clientele seemed different than the norm. The median age dropped by about ten points when I met a guy in his forties, his younger wife and their infant son. The family had joined the cruise at the beginning, back in Turkey, and were staying aboard for three weeks. I hypothesized that the baby was a prop and the couple were on the lam. Nobody but a retiree stays on a river cruise for three weeks, and nobody in their right mind drags along a squalling toddler.

But, this guy didn't seem to have a care in the world. He never mentioned having a job, and he didn't have the shifty eyes of a bank robber or the charming charisma of an international jewel thief. He just smiled, laughed and told me that he'd also brought his mother along for the ride. She would be joining them in a few minutes.

My first thought was that he was either a slightly goofy dot-com millionaire or a lottery winner who loved his elderly mother. It was kind of nice, thinking that this fellow had invited his mom on a sight-seeing trip. As a fringe benefit, I figured her job was to watch the baby while the couple haggled for doodads in the local markets, dined on numerous variations of goat parts, sucked down exotic drinks and made condescending remarks about the indigenous accent.

Cougar Grandma

My theory was turned on its head when I met Grandma. I'm not sure if anyone has yet coined the term for a seventy-two-year-old cougar. The only thing that comes to mind is "GILF," and the very thought of that makes me a trifle nauseous. She'd enjoy that definition, but I'd prefer to stick to the under-forty crowd.

At any rate, Granny was a player. She didn't hesitate to tell me how she was seventy-two, but didn't look or feel a day over fifty. This, she further explained, was thanks to a steady diet of face-lifts, tucks, Botox, liposuction and collagen injections. She displayed not a hint of embarrassment in over-sharing the details of her various procedures with a total stranger. After I survived her opening salvo of unwanted detail, the only thing that surprised me was that she wasn't wearing leopard-print spandex and an Aerosmith T-shirt.

I'll admit that Granny didn't look her age. In fact, she didn't really look any age. Her skin was stretched tighter than Bernie Madoff's checking account. She had a permanently implanted smile that reminded me of either the Joker or Elizabeth Dole. I saw no lines, wrinkles, freckles or age spots. Drop a quarter on that face and it would have bounced two-feet high.

Granny had endless stories, most of them about herself. In a classic case of "too much information," she informed me that she had recently jettisoned her latest boy toy...thirty years her junior. Staring deeply and attempting to make with the doe-eyes (no small feat when your face has been winched back so often that your gaze is slightly reminiscent of Ming the Merciless), she claimed that this former boyfriend was both heartbroken and lonely. She had moved on, but according to her, he was having a difficult time transitioning to his next love.

Several thoughts passed through my head as she droned on, not the least of which was the most expedient way to extricate myself from further conversation with Zsa Zsa the Bore. I wondered if her recently departed boyfriend spelled his last name "Gigolo." I wondered just how many plastic surgeons were the proud owners of an S-class Mercedes thanks to this Geritol-spouting fountain of lost youth. I'm almost certain that, if a Barbie doll experienced some sort of Pygmalion-esque transformation, she would sound just like this old gal.

What I didn't wonder about was the reason that Granny and her family were spending a not-so-small fortune on a three-week river cruise through Europe. Granny was loaded. She confirmed my certainty when her son blurted out that he acted as the family's money manager.. I have always believed that money can't buy happiness, but this chance meeting did teach me that it can buy your kid a job and the type of brand-new plastic face that makes the toy designers at Mattel drool with both fear and envy.

Wertheim Is for Glass

This family would play a larger role in my journey, but we'll save that for later. Some recollections can be digested only in small doses, with a hefty dollop of Maalox on the side. There were actually a number of pleasant stops along the trip. One of my favorites was in the city of Wertheim.

Wertheim is loaded with glass shops, the type of place where a bull running amuck would have a field day. The town was once the home to industrial glass shops that created the items more recognizable in a lab than some storefront knick-knack establishment. As that industry became more automated, these incredible artisans and glass blowers of unsurpassed skill found a new way to make money and showcase their skills. To reach their absolute full potential one might have to wait until somebody figures out how to integrate a glass-blowing program into a Wii or an Xbox 360. Still, the glasswork you'll find in Wertheim is excellent. The local craftsmen create everything from Christmas ornaments to massive glass sculptures to shot glasses adorned with the logo "I visited Wertheim and all I got was a buzz."

Tourists, and the river cruises that bring them, have single handedly revived towns like Wertheim. The disappearance of industry and military bases—for decades the primary employers—threw many of these towns into a depression that was immune to the healing effects of cutting-edge pharmaceuticals. No test tube makers or Army guys meant that few people had money to spend on crystal busts of the Bronnback abbé. That all changed thanks to what has become a booming river cruise market. The ships bring in hordes of tourists on a daily basis, and travelers are treated wonderfully.

Visiting a glass blowing workshop in Wertheim, Germany.

It's a symbiotic relationship. The various communities literally open their arms to those who are ready to open their wallets.

At each stop, after a day spent exploring the town and subsidizing the local economy, the river cruisers reboard the ship for dinner and some entertainment in the lounge. That entertainment almost always consists of a piano player or singer. Thankfully, lederhosen-bedecked accordion players tend to keep their distance.

Martinis and Missiles

On this particular cruise the traditional musical interlude was usually superseded by Granny's trust-fund son and his laptop computer. Every night Sonny staked out his favorite stool at the bar as if it were the most sought-after gold claim in the Yukon. He flipped open the laptop, turned up the volume and watched grainy videos. We all thought he was playing some sort of futuristic war game, which is just about what you'd expect from a forty-year-old man-child whose neck bears the scars of titanium apron strings. Our suppositions couldn't have been further from the truth.

Sonny, it turned out, was a wannabe warrior. His face broke out in a huge and disconcerting grin as he explained to the Hungarian bartender that he was watching actual footage of American Apache helicopters in Iraq. Somehow, and this is proof positive that too much money is not good in the hands of folks who are addle-brained, he had obtained classified videos stolen by the WikiLeaks folks.

To say that the videos were disturbing would be a gross understatement. Our resident lunatic had obviously watched these films a few thousand times, and he provided play-by-play and color commentary for every person in the bar. Like a prop comic with only a single rubber chicken, Sonny offered the exact same gory stories night after night.

Word soon spread, with the result being that the lounge became about as popular as Death Valley in August. The clientele generally consisted of our hawkish video addict, my crew, the bartender and the poor dude who was banging out some off-key Billy Joel to a large and empty lounge. It's really quite amazing that Sonny managed to find a wife, let alone have a child. You don't expect a guy like that to ever leave the basement or change out of his footie pajamas.

It was a strange contrast. A quiet and relaxing trip down the scenic rivers of Europe combined with war videos. If there was any silver lining to the story, it was that horny Granny was never seen in the ship's bar. I don't know if she found a new boyfriend, or if her kid's behavior surpassed even her stratospheric bar of inappropriate behavior.

My crew and I had a low tolerance for Sonny, and generally retired to our respective rooms after a couple of quick drinks. We'd try to banish his graphic video descriptions from our minds, catch a few winks, and prepare to explore the sights and sounds of the next day's village.

I do feel sorry for the Hungarian bartender who had no place to go until the "war games" guy got bored or his battery died. Plastic granny should have at least offered to pay for his therapy. Her strange offspring could drive Mother Teresa to cuss like a longshoreman. That bartender is going to be on a psychiatrist's couch for years.

Siegfried's Mechanical Beasts

As the days passed by our cruise stopped in a number of different villages down river. One of these was a small place known as Rudesheim, a winemaking town that sits along the Rhine. The town has a long history, not the least of which is that it was the subject of British musician David Garrick's 1970 hit "Rüdesheim liegt nicht an der Themse" ("Rüdesheim Does Not Lie on the Thames"). Now there's something you won't learn in your average German history class. Somewhere, Casey Kasem is weeping.

We reached Rudesheim near the end of the river-cruising season. The sky was as gray as the inside of a pewter mug, something that seemed to be in surprisingly short supply for a town whose fortunes rested on retail sales of the fruit of the vine. The doors of many of the restaurants and pubs were locked. Proprietors were preparing to close up after a prosperous season, looking forward to some winter rest. You know your trip is winding down when a town known for its wine consumption puts up a month's long "last call" sign.

The one thing that wasn't winding down was a little museum a few blocks from the river. That's where we discovered Siegfried's Mechanical Museum. Siegfried's was just winding up.

The owner of the museum was Siegfried Wendel, and no, he didn't have a partner named Roy. Most people would consider Siegfried to be a bit on the eccentric side, and most people would be right. He had all the makings of a world-class mad scientist... the Einstein hair, the rumpled clothes and the twenty-inch-thick Andy Rooney eyebrows. You overlooked all this as soon as Siegfried fires up one of his mechanical beasts. It was a bit of a chore to convince this master of mechanical mayhem to do that—such was part of his charm—but for some reason he decided we were worthy acolytes.

Where the hell are my elves?

Siegfried, without the tigers (or elves), and his magical machines.

Siegfried didn't speak very much English and I don't speak any German. This probably smoothed matters, as his machines communicated just fine on their own.

The contraptions in Siegfried's museum ranged from hand-cranked music boxes to a gigantic, concert piano orchestrion. Some fit in the palm of your hand; some were the size of a country singer's RV. Better yet, all the devices were scattered throughout a fifteenth-century castle. Every single one was lovingly restored by Siegfried. This included a truly amazing piece known as "Bernhard Dufner's Band of 27 Automatic Dolls."

This is a bit difficult to describe. Think along the lines of Chuckie meets the Glenn Miller Orchestra and drops the butcher knife. The mechanical dolls all banged out their tunes on different instruments. You'd be seriously impressed, and you'd also leave with a significant amount of hearing loss.

Which, in this case, is not such a bad thing. Upon leaving Siegfried's museum you exit onto Drosselgasse, the main thoroughfare and most famous street in Rudesheim. This street comes to life at around noon, and remains a hot spot well into the wee hours of the morning. Even though Rudesheim was on the verge on shutting down for the season, the locals would soon be sampling their personal stash of fermented wares. The proverbial joint might still have a few jumps left in it before things came to a halt.

Unfortunately, those jumps will come with the sound of oompah bands. I suppose we should have appreciated this aspect of local culture, and I'm well aware that patience is a virtue.

But sometimes, and you'll just have to trust me on this, temporary deafness can be a blessing.

3

Buddy the Sheep

Do you have kids? Have you ever been a kid? Well, the answer to one or both of these questions has to be a "yes." Do you tell your kids stories or were you told stories when you were a child? My mom was a great storyteller as I got older, but my dad was the main storyteller when I was a kid. I always heard a variation of the three pigs as they went out on different adventures. The main characters might have stayed the same, but the stories always had a different twist. It was necessary to keep us engaged and enthralled as each night we'd hear a new story of the pigs and how they avoided disaster at the hands of the big bad wolf.

I've taken this same approach to my two children, entertaining them with colorful yarns with my own twist.

Because I travel so much, I make it a point to spend as much quality time as possible with my children. Part of that happens at bedtime when I carry on the tradition with stories that mix family members, the kids themselves and other random characters that the kids especially enjoy. For instance, Clifford the Big Red Dog or Dora the Explorer have shown up in various stories to assist in saving a friend or taking them on an adventure. Some have even included flying dragons that would help my kids rescue their friends from danger.

On the night before I left on a trip to Wales I started to tell a story about my adventures there. My kids weren't part of that one, but it still had that strong fantasy angle that I constructed for their maximum delight. Unfortunately, this time I think I got in a bit over my head.

I told my daughter that the next night, as she was sleeping, my plane would be racing across the sky to a different country, a land known as Wales that had more sheep than people. I told her I was destined to meet a particular sheep, a sheep named Buddy, who would make a connection with me. As the plane I was on flew over the green pastures of Wales on its approach to Cardiff, this sheep named Buddy would look up and realize that he was destined to meet someone on that plane. That someone was me!

I explained to her that Buddy was no ordinary sheep. Indeed, Buddy was the only talking sheep in all of Wales. He had special powers that made him more human than animal and he was prepared to not only find me somehow, but to show me his country. This, I explained, was one of the reasons I was traveling there.

I knew my general itinerary, but not what we would be shooting per se, so I was generous in my descriptions and ideas for what we would encounter. My little girl looked up at me with tired yet intense eyes as she hung on every word. I couldn't read her mind, but if I could I could just imagine the wheels spinning as she considered the possibility of a talking sheep hanging out with her dad. How cool, she must have been thinking.

The Taiwanese Infiltrator

The next day we headed off to Wales and literally hit the ground running. After a shower and quick change at the country inn where we were staying we headed into Cardiff. Even though Cardiff is a city, it's small by the standards you might be accustomed to in the United States, especially those along the coasts. But that's why we travel to places like Wales. We love to show you their cities and even their smaller villages, giving you an insight into their local culture and experiences.

The afternoon started out at the Wales Millennium Centre. Completed in 2005, this building was designed to reflect the many different parts of the country, with local Welsh materials that dominate its history: slate, metal, wood and glass. The building itself was constructed from 1,350 tons of Welsh slate, 300,000 concrete blocks and a million meters of electric cable.

It's a beautiful structure in a great setting. This part of Cardiff is right on the bay, and right next to the old Pierhead building, a French Gothic Renaissance–style edifice also known as Baby Big Ben because of its signature clock tower. The day we were there a small fair had taken over this great retail and cultural area that overlooks the water. We tried some local foods and even played a local game that was created in Wales.

An overview of Cardiff, Wales.

At one point Nick took off to shoot some B-roll around the area—scenic and atmospheric material that we would use to supplement the primary shots of me touring and talking. I had already taken care of my part and all Nick had to do was spend about twenty minutes getting a variety of shots and we'd be ready to pack up and head out.

Thirty minutes later there was no sign of Nick. At forty-five minutes I began to wonder if he had fallen into the water and drowned, as Nick cannot swim. Before I became too worried about his potential drowning, I saw two men walking toward me with Nick sandwiched between them. They weren't two random people escorting him, but actual police. Oh boy, I thought, what has Nick done?

Of course, Nick is the last guy to cause any trouble, so I wasn't really too worried, but I *was* curious. I learned later that these guys had witnessed Nick taking a variety of videos all over the area with his professional gear. He certainly stood out in this setting considering that Nick is Taiwanese and there aren't too many Taiwanese people running around with $7,000 cameras shooting video at Welsh fairs.

The constables had approached Nick and questioned him about what he was doing and why. He told them that we were working with Wales Tourism to capture aspects of the destination. They listened to that answer and proceeded to take him upstairs to an office where another individual asked him the same questions. When Nick explained that he was there to film and had written permission to do that they asked the next logical question. "Where's the document?" That document was sitting in one of the bags I was guarding, and that's why I now stood obediently with Nick and the two policemen, who waited patiently as he fished out the letter from the tourism department. Things were quickly resolved and we headed out.

Later that evening I called home and told my wife about the day's events, including Nick's short-term confinement. She barely got a laugh out when my daughter anxiously got on the phone and started to ask me about Buddy. She wanted to know if I had seen him yet, what he had said, where we were going and more. I told her I had yet to see him, but it was only my first day. Rest assured I said, he's here and he's looking for me. It's only a matter of time.

Don't Call Me Buddy

By the third day in Wales I knew I was in trouble. My daughter was unrelenting as she pressed me for information on Buddy. I eventually broke down and told her what I knew was my responsibility to disclose that we had encountered him that day and he was now traveling with us and showing us around. "Put him on the phone" she stated, "I want to speak to him."

She was at that age when she questioned everything and was definitely under the impression that I was trying to pull a fast one on her. I wanted the magic to continue as my little girl would be little only a bit longer and moments like these are truly precious.

As she pressed me I did some quick thinking and explained that it was already bedtime in Wales even though it was still daytime in New Jersey. I told her that Buddy was already sound asleep and I didn't want to wake or bother him just as I wouldn't wake or bother her if she was sleeping.

This was met by silence; silence that indicated she thought I might be full of it. I finally got an "Okay, but I want to talk to him…" I told her not to worry; I'll be getting Buddy on camera so she'd be able to hear him talk when I make it home.

I turned to my guide the next day and explained my dilemma.

"Mary, we need to find a talking sheep."

She looked at me with an odd expression and said "Excuse me?"

I shared my story and what I had promised to my daughter and watched her face change again. I think she thought I was daft, or at least some kind of practical joker. I am the second, but in this case I was completely serious and told her why.

"I would really like a chance to get up close to one so we can create a little short film," I told her.

Did I really want to get close to a sheep so I could "talk to it" she asked. "Yes," I replied to her look of disbelief. No doubt that look of disbelief had more to do with how difficult that task was actually going to be versus the request itself.

Maybe she gets a lot of requests from tourists who want to talk to sheep…or maybe not. I was about to find out just how difficult it might be for me to fulfill the promise of my story to my daughter.

Even though the country is full of sheep, getting close to one is a real challenge. They want nothing to do with you if they don't know you, and maybe less if they do, and quickly run the other way. (You can go ahead and insert your own personal joke here.)

Even if you have food you might be out of luck. They are nervous little guys and gals. I went from enjoying the views from the car of the rolling green hills to being in "sheep alert" mode. Well, it's not exactly *sheep alert* mode as there are sheep everywhere you turn. Most aren't near the road itself, though, so I was yelling out to stop anytime I saw a stray one close to a fence or near the side of the road.

Mary would quickly pull over and indulge my desire to talk to one of these sheep. It was a complete failure each time as the sheep wouldn't wait for us to get close before scampering away quickly. We'd jump out and scramble to grab the microphone and camera only to have the sheep skedaddle before we were even within twenty yards.

This is going to be tough, I thought. And not just in getting up close to the mangy little buggers. What about the whole idea of the sheep talking? I hadn't even considered that aspect of what I was trying to do as I was completely consumed by simply trying to find one to stand still for a few seconds.

You might be thinking, how do you get a sheep to talk? The reality is much simpler. Just get close enough to stick a microphone near its mouth and let editing take care of the rest. Unfortunately, scattering sheep met attempt after attempt as we traveled from seaside towns in the south to the hills and slate mines of the north.

The owner operators of the establishments where we stayed cook gourmet meals for their guests. The food was great, but there was a big downside. They were all located in what most people would consider the middle of nowhere. You had the proprietor and, if lucky, one or two other guests. The average age of these other guests made these places feel more like God's waiting room than a place to go on holiday.

Our sheep encounter was looking futile until our last stop, a cottage that happened to be on a sheep farm in the north. For the first time we had a dining room with plenty of local people, including a television personality, and a taste of the national dish—lamb. We had passed on it all week, but finally broke down and dined on a wonderfully prepared dish. While I was complementing our hosts on a fantastic meal—mutton, as I recall—I asked if they could arrange for us to interview one of their sheep.

I'm not sure they had ever heard this request, and not unlike Mary, gave me what could only be described as a strange look. The look that asks, "Is this some kind of joke...?"

When I shared my story they were understanding and encouraged me to visit the sheep pen first thing in the morning. I explained the challenges over the past few days and they assured me that carrying a small bowl into the pen would make the sheep think I was there to feed them, bringing them closer and giving me a chance to complete my task.

Doing Hard Time in the Pen

Now, my idea of a sheep pen was something small that would give me easy access to the animals and a way to corner one of them into hamming it up for the camera—or, at least standing still for a minute so we could get our shots and do our thing. Unfortunately, that wasn't going to be the case. The pen was quite large and the sheep had seen me coming and moved to the other side at the outset. The food charade had zero effect, as they showed no interest in me or what was in the little bowl.

There was an added obstacle I hadn't considered when climbing over the fence into the sheep pen with my empty little plate—sheep droppings. They were everywhere. As I tried to gracefully approach the pack of sheep I was anything but graceful. My halting steps added to the stress the sheep must have already been feeling as most of them scurried in the other direction. They must have thought they were being stalked, for indeed they were!

Just as I thought there was no way this would ever work, one of the sheep, heretofore known as Buddy, stopped and turned his head toward us. With the camera rolling I started in on my commentary and everything came into sync. It was as if he was actually listening to us and in agreement with what I said! Maybe this was truly Buddy the Sheep and I hadn't made up the story in my head as part of some fantasy for my child. Maybe, just maybe, I had actually channeled Buddy's thoughts and simply foretold the future…All right—maybe I just got lucky and the sheep stopped and turned. The sheep was clear across the pen at this point and not coming closer, but the zoom lens made it possible for us to capture this moment for my little girl. My luck wasn't going to last much longer.

As I turned to ask Nick if he was able to get it he had a twisted expression on his face. He said, "I have to go." I replied, "We both have to go," meaning head out from the property and get on our way to Manchester and our flight back home. He reiterated, "No, I really have to go," turned around and went over the fence leaving the camera behind for me to bring back.

What was up with Nick? I've been plenty of places and Nick always seems to come down with something. Suddenly it dawned on me. Nick had just been struck by "Buddy's Revenge," similar in size and scope to Montezuma's Revenge made famous in trips to Mexico. I started to laugh until a feint gurgle started in my stomach signaling a wave of contractions that were soon to start. I barely made it back to the room and my bathroom before it struck me as well.

Buddy, or so our theory goes, was acting out to avenge the death of one of his brothers. That brother must have been served up the night before in complete disagreement to both of our digestive systems the next day. It took a few false starts, but we finally made it back downstairs and on our way.

This last segment we captured in Wales is what became known as Buddy's Adventure: The story of a talking sheep and his journey from Wales to America. You might be asking yourself "how did Buddy learn this incredible skill?" The secret behind Buddy's ability to talk, as the story goes, was based on the fact that aliens had captured him and they had made this possible. Up until the point where I met Buddy he had remained silent for fear of being ostracized from his brothers and sisters in the pen. That is, until we showed up and liberated Buddy from his silence and freed him from any constraints. Go Buddy!

Buddy the Sheep gets adopted.

4

Unscripted Food Adventures in Spain

You gotta love Spain and Spaniards. The food is fabulous, and the adventures you can have in trying to experience the country's culinary delights can at times border on the edgy, sort of like running insanely down an ancient street a few feet ahead of stampeding bulls. This is what happens when dealing with complex travel logistics, schmoozing with the locals, setting up scenes and then actually consuming the victuals with the camera running. It would be easy to say that the unscripted experiences that occur so easily here are a reflection of the Spanish national personality, but the truth is that we deal with the same escapades wherever we go.

In fact, we have to leap crazy hurdles on almost every one of our trips in order to shoot what we need or capture a particular aspect of a destination or product. A well-meaning individual typically puts the hurdle in place. It's usually the person assigned to helping us coordinate a particular trip, but one that might not understand what needs to happen for us to get the job done while we are on the road. It's why we prefer to handle our own arrangements and not be part of any group or anyone else's particular agenda.

On one recent trip to Spain, one that was scheduled months in advance, we received our final itinerary only the day before we left. Such last-minuteness boggles the mind, but again, this is pretty typical of what happens as we try to plan our adventures. I've been known to show up at the airport where I'm met by a representative waving a stained, printed document outlining a two-week trip. Believe it or not, up to that point we often are still unsure of many of the stops, special opportunities or even the hotels where we will be staying.

When this happens it means that yet again we will be traveling unscripted, but it's not that bad because it obviously feeds into our entire concept of just letting unexpected things happen. This way of working has become a challenge, but it's also our hallmark. A suggestion by a guide may lead us to a special bar or market, and next thing you know we are putting together something completely different than what we originally thought would have occurred.

This dynamic played out when we traveled to Spain's Andalucia region, where we were scheduled to visit three places: Malaga, Seville and Ronda. We planned to spend at least two nights in each location to help us gather our thoughts and ideas for capturing a particular experience or aspect of travel to a city or town.

When the company that was sponsoring our trip originally put it together, they had us staying in a different place each night and traveling part of every day. We had to explain that this wasn't feasible if we were to shoot content and not simply "tour." Apparently they felt the more they could jam in, the more we could shoot, the better for them and the destination. We corrected these misconceptions and narrowed our focus down to those three locations.

Yes, We Have No Oranges

On our first stop we were doing a final wrap of the beach community just outside of Malaga, a destination known as Torremolinos, when we ran into an orange shortage. Well, it wasn't exactly an orange shortage given the number of orange trees all over this part of Spain. It was more like a ladder shortage, as you'll notice in the video.

In the wrap to this segment I was trying to tie in something a little different, an interesting tidbit about the trees on a particular street. The oranges you see on these trees aren't eaten in the conventional way as they aren't very good to the taste. Instead, they are used to make a marmalade that's sold throughout the area.

A Charlie Sheen moment.

We decided that I would speak to the camera about the oranges and how they were used while I pulled one off the tree to illustrate my point. Then I would simply turn and walk off camera as it faded to black. Sounds pretty easy, right? Something that should have been quite simple became a real pain in the ass. That's just how it goes sometimes in our world.

As I started to speak one thing after another created an interruption. It was sometimes a loud truck going by, or just me screwing up, and in other cases I mistook my sound guy doing something with his hand as a signal to stop. To make matters worse, each time I shot it I had to pull an orange from a tree branch on the street.

Pretty soon, I'd done so many takes that there were no more oranges on the tree, at least ones that were in reach. Indeed, one of my takes went perfectly until I reached up to grab an orange for the final emphasis, and then...I couldn't reach it! That's right, it was about two inches away from my hand as I extended and stretched as far as I could. *"Son of a bitch!"* I finally had to resort to wedging an already picked orange between two branches and hope that no one would notice.

We finally wrapped that segment as the sun was setting and headed to our hotel for a well-deserved dinner and night's sleep. Our next stop would be Seville.

On the drive from Malaga to Seville the next day, roughly two and half hours away, our guide informed us that the second hotel's location was forty-five minutes outside of Seville. This surprised our team as we were under the impression that we'd be spending time in Seville to shoot content and would stay in one of the many hotels there. We are never sure how a day might go and

The city of Torresmolinos, west of Malaga.

frequently need to change for different segments, so the idea of a forty-five-minute drive to our "base" was out of the question.

When hearing this we immediately reached out to our sponsor and asked for a change. The answer came back that our guide was available to drive us anywhere and at any time of the day or night. Unfortunately, this had nothing at all to do with the root problem.

When we are filming a destination or telling a story about one we don't go in a linear path. We might shoot the middle and end of a segment and then come back and shoot the beginning later that day or even the next day. We are very opportunistic and take advantage of serendipity as it happens. It comes down to flexibility, something that staying so far away from the location would make impossible.

Think about it. Would I transport my clothes in the car from the hotel and change on the street or in the car itself? Better yet, park at a hotel and sneak into their bathroom to change? I don't think so.

Then again, maybe…especially considering my Type-A impatience. As we awaited a legitimate answer to our request, I impulsively made an executive decision and grabbed clothes to make two changes during the day in a local hotel bathroom. I had our guide clear it with their front desk, so everything was copasetic. I just couldn't imagine having to do this for the next two days.

As the day wore on, and as no answers came back to move us to a new base hotel, I decided to just take command. After all, I'm not a wait-around type of guy.

So, I stepped up to the plate, took the reins, slid into the driver's seat, got on the horse, grabbed the Spanish bull by the horns (insert your favorite metaphor here) and did what was necessary. I booked us into a Seville hotel. Sure, the expense was moved from the tour guide to me, but it meant that we'd be able to do what we had to do. Because I had absolutely no idea of when I'd next be in Seville with a camera crew, I was intent on making sure that we made the most of this particular stay. We were roughly a ten-minute walk into the historic area. We'd be able to adapt to any opportunity that might make itself available, so I figured it was well worth the money.

The Joy of Tapas

As part of our minimal preparations for Spain we decided that a tapas eating montage would be part of the mix. Tapas is a finger food that's best eaten with others. It's a big part of the Spanish culture and one of the reasons foodies love the country. Some tapas are very straightforward, like cured ham and cheese—and this country eats a ton of ham. Indeed, for those of you who believe in reincarnation, be forewarned that if you screw up in this life your punishment might be showing up in the next life as a pig in Spain. Let's just say it would be a short visit.

In one sitting you can sample a fantastic variety of these small dishes and do it all over some great wine. That's one of the cool things about travel and food. Both bring people together. We were able to do this in each of the cities we explored spending time with everyone from college students to travel guides to local teachers. They all played a role in our unscripted adventures.

We also tried plenty of other little bites, including meatballs with French fries, some other parts of the pig, lamb and a dish made of rice. The most adventurous thing I saw looked more like bean sprouts to me than what they really were: eels.

Unless you looked really closely you wouldn't even notice that they were eels. My sound guy Gene Kang didn't know what they were until he ate one. The texture tipped him off as he expected it to be crunchy, like a bean sprout, which didn't turn out to be the case.

When your brain doesn't connect to what your mouth is actually processing, a phenomenon occurs known scientifically as mind/mouth confusion, abbreviated in some medical journals as "WTF!?" You are momentarily suspended in a sort of confused limbo as your brain begins to process what's going on, sending frantic signals to your stomach. In the case of Gene, those signals were something akin to "Code Blue!" Gene won't even eat everyday seafood, so he wasn't too thrilled about downing this little treat.

We tried to get different people together, in the different places we visited, to try some tapas with them. Our first stop in Malaga

Those are baby eels...not bean sprouts!

Our new friends in Malaga...before things turned weird.

resulted in me sitting with several twenty-something women who were willing to work with us and share their insights. It was a fun opening to this part of our adventure, although the adventure continued after the cameras were put away.

When we finished filming our segment with the willing participants at the tapas restaurant, they offered to take us to a different place. Wanting to be immersed in the local culture we accepted their offer, only to learn that two out of the three had to pack it in for the night. That left us with the one lady who became our pied piper and led us to the next eatery. She mentioned meeting up with some friends and we simply followed along. Two of her friends met us at the next stop and we became part of a larger strategic plan that seemed to take shape quickly after we sat down.

That plan would include the molestation of our producer, Nick. It's rare for guys to be viewed as prey, but that's exactly what started to happen. As we ordered more food and drinks the girl closest to Nick made her move. She seamlessly reached under the table and squeezed his leg.

You have to understand Nick and to have actually had the experience of poking him once or twice to know why this caused a reaction akin to a seizure. A gentle nudge in the side will have him launching off a chair or jumping out of his shoes. This guy is touchy!

As her hand closed around his thigh you can imagine what happened next. Nick almost sprang out of his seat. His arms flew out from his sides and his body convulsed as his face took on an incredulous expression. It was priceless. It was akin to an epileptic chicken flapping its wings.

While this was going on I was speaking with the girl who had been part of our segment. She was nice enough and quite young as it turned out. She was still in college and her parents were in their forties, just like me! I was lucky that I chose this seat to sit in because it gave me a great view of Nick and his new "friend."

The best part of this whole evening was watching Nick. It was all I could do to not appear rude or distracted, but distracted I was. Here's a guy who is extremely shy, and one who wouldn't consider hanging out with some random girl in a foreign country, much less getting his leg massaged under the table.

The small space in which we sat made it next to impossible for Nick to move beyond a few inches, bumping into Gene's leg in his desire to escape the probing fingers of his newfound friend.

Nick wasn't relaxed at this point. He was more like an alert Doberman. You can spot them when their ears perk up and their nose probes the air as they try to figure out what's happening around them. Nick was definitely on full alert and not too happy about it. Even if he were single, this was not someone Nick would be interested in. The fact that he's married and sooooo not interested made for a funny and entertaining soirée.

So here I am watching this interaction and Nick's uncomfortable expression and I'm practically laughing out loud. The more uncomfortable he seemed, the funnier it became. I found myself looking away to keep myself in check, because no one other than Nick and I seemed to know what was going on at that particular moment.

And then it happened. It was like slow-motion car wreck. Time slowed down and the sound around me became muted as I watched "Nick's Girl" pick up a handful of napkins with one hand

and pull her sleeve to the side with the other. In a coordinated move she reached across her chest and found her target. The napkins completed the sweep of her armpit, wiping the excess sweat away in a series of back and forth moves.

In a word...GROSS! The moist napkins found themselves back on the table as she picked up another bunch and proceeded to attack her other armpit. Wow. Talk about disgusting. I went from hysterical laughter that was testing all of my abilities of restraint, to complete and utter disgust—all at the sight of what I had just witnessed.

Nick's horrific expression made it clear that he saw the same thing I did. The realization was all too clear as the hand covered with warm pit juice landed back on his leg. In the annals of pick up strategies this one had to go down as one of the most bizarre as well as most unsuccessful I have ever seen.

Hey...it was just another evening of *Travel Unscripted*. Now pass the tapas, *por favor*!

5

Vietnam Unscripted

Traveling to Asia from the east coast of America can make you crazy, especially when nubile young women, booze and some serious jet lag are involved.

Just hear me out on this one, and please don't jump to any conclusions—at least not right away.

It all started when I last traveled to Vietnam, flying from Newark to Taipei, with a stop in Anchorage to refuel and take on a new crew. As usual, I was with my trusty chief videographer and traveling companion, Nick Choo.

Once in Taipei we spent several hours in the business class lounge as we waited for our connection to Ho Chi Minh City, or Saigon as some still call it. While there, Nick and I did some people watching, one of my favorite things to do when I travel. I still marvel at how we can travel halfway around the world in hours and be exposed to so many different cultures, where people are so different in some ways and yet so similar in others.

Aviation Lust

While we bided our time, one fellow traveler in particular stood out. She was young, Asian and extremely attractive, wearing a form-fitting dress. She stood about 5'4" tall, but the heels she had on put her closer to 5'8". Her large brown eyes looked straight ahead as her long dark hair bounced off her shoulders. She had us mesmerized as she glided through the lounge. Her full lips were unusual, as was her overall look. I imagined her parents to be of different races and to have formed this beautiful woman who strolled confidently through the lounge as if she owned it.

Necks were definitely craning...at least until she took her leave of the premises. Or sooner, if one of those craning their necks received a stern look by his female traveling companion, or worse, a crack to the side of the head. I was safe with Nick at my side as I enjoyed this nice diversion.

Two hours later, when the airline called our flight, Nick and I packed up our computers and started to head out. With the attention span of gnats we had already forgotten the woman in the lounge and had rallied for the final leg of our trip to Vietnam. That changed when the object of our admiration suddenly reappeared just as we were exiting. She flashed us a big smile and we responded like Pavlov's dogs with smiles of our own. Both of us were grinning from ear to ear as we made our way to the gate.

As we walked toward our plane I decided to take a little detour to check out some shops in the airport. Nick went on and a few minutes passed before I caught up with him again. When I eventually walked into the gate area I immediately noticed that Nick was waiting far from the crowds and had a lone person sitting alongside him: the woman from the lounge!

As I walked over to Nick I put a twisted expression of concern on my face and turned to the unsuspecting woman. As she looked up and made eye contact I asked her in a halting way "Are-you-following-us???"

With nothing short of a look of bewilderment she let out an "Absolutely not!"

That was the first time I heard her voice which spoke in slightly accented, but seemingly fluent English. "What are you, some kind of stalker?" I added.

This was met by an even more incredulous look as she laughed nervously and said "No, who are you anyway?"

Before she darted for airport security I decided to tell her that I was simply having some fun at her expense. I'm not sure she initially knew what to make of my silliness, but it sure was worth the effort, as the look on her face was absolutely priceless. So with my gag over and the preboarding being announced, we grabbed some of our equipment, said goodbye and headed for the plane. I thought this would be our last encounter, but again I was mistaken.

As we settled into our seats the same woman came onboard and took her assigned seat—right in front of us! I'm guessing it was her bad day!

Being no fool, at this point I took the opportunity to formally introduce myself and apologize for my earlier antics. She was gracious and actually seemed to be amused by the whole episode. She said her name was My Linh, explaining that she was a naturalized American citizen who moved from Vietnam to the United States in 1990. She still retained her accent and a deep knowledge of Vietnam and in particular Ho Chi Minh City. She was on her way back from the States as she spent most of her time in Vietnam managing a restaurant.

Because we literally "show up and shoot" at locations around the world, I usually seek out someone in the destination to provide insights and color. It could be a vendor on the street, a taxi driver, or in the case of this flight, My Linh. This was my chance to get a head start on the process because I would have only a few hours later that afternoon to shoot, and we didn't have anybody working with us on this trip. We were scheduled to leave the hotel early the next day to jump on a river cruise to Siem Reap, giving us a fleeting opportunity to capture something unique about the city.

With a tight window to accomplish our goal, I did my best to gather as many ideas from our new travel buddy and she was willing to oblige.

Later, as our three-hour flight from Taipei to Ho Chi Minh City was about to end, My Linh invited Nick and me to join her and some friends that evening, assuming we weren't too tired by then. She was taking a group out to celebrate a birthday, something I honestly would never imagine doing immediately after twenty-four hours of travel. However, I guess her many charms got the better of us, so we took her phone number and told her that we would do our best to connect later on.

Rickshaw Shakedown

The prospect of going out with My Linh appeared to be an absolutely awful option a few hours later when we dragged our asses in from a hot day of being ridden all over the city on a cycle rickshaw where the driver sits behind you and you ride in front on a seat.

Allow me to digress for a minute as I admit that the little rick-shaw ride had beaten the hell out of me—both emotionally and physically. You see, after we got out of the airport we found two guys with these classic Asian vehicles by the post office that showcases some of the French influence in Vietnam. That was our starting-out point, so we made a deal with them to cart us around this part of the city.

Being veteran travelers, I thought we did a good job of clarify-ing the fee we'd pay for the few hours that they'd be taking us around. Yet what I learned through this little exercise was that you might want to see something in writing before you commit to anything in a foreign land. Better yet, it's a good idea to work through a travel agent for any kind of travel plans. They know the ropes and can help you avoid what happened to me. (You'd think I, of all people, would have known better!)

This driver might look like he's twelve, but he knows how to score a few bucks.

If you do what Mark says and not what Mark does (or did!), you should be able to avoid this embarrassing and painful problem: The rickshaw dude told me was that the cost was $3 an hour for each driver. What he didn't share with me until later was the "chart" that he handily kept hidden somewhere in his rickety vehicle, which stated a fee of *$20 an hour*. So, after our little tour, as we stood on the side of an alley near our hotel and tried to settle up, my originally generous tip was shunned, as it wasn't a fraction of the money these hucksters were actually seeking. The guy who did the initial bargaining suddenly had a bad case of amnesia with regard to our initial conversation.

I knew I was being taken like some kind of rookie tourist and I had to laugh. Here I am a very seasoned travel pro and a tag team in a rickshaw works me over for a total of $120! To put that number in perspective, the average wage in this particular city for a professional working one or more jobs can be about $200 a month.

I'd say that these rickshaw guys made out okay in their fleecing. At least I could take some solace in the fact that this amount of money meant a lot more to them and their day-to-day lives than to me. I decided to call it an extra donation and a learning experience, albeit a forced one.

A Second Wind for Ho Chi Minh

But what about lovely My Linh? Well, night was closing in and after the rickshaw experience we were feeling beat. Still, we decided to rally and go outside the hotel to eat at a nice restaurant. Halfway through dinner we both struggled to not fall into our plates. We were fading fast and had decided that the local scene, no matter how fun it might be, would have to wait. We were dead in our seats at 9:00 p.m.

That all changed as we were getting our check thirty minutes later, when suddenly we were wide awake and ready to party.

You might be asking how things could change so quickly? It's called "jet lag" and it has a terrible habit of keeping you up when you want to sleep and making you sleepy when you need to be alert. When you travel to places like Vietnam from the east coast of the United States you are on the opposite end of the clock. Eleven o'clock in the evening there is actually 11:00 in the morning back home.

What got us going was that exact dynamic. It was 10:00 p.m. when I picked up the phone to take My Linh up on her offer, making it more like 9:00 a.m. to us. In my foolish second-wind-edness I went ahead and sent her a text that we'd love to meet up. A moment later my phone buzzed from that number she had provided along with this message: "Huh?"

Had she given us a fake number? I showed the phone to Nick and laughed. Murphy's law, of course. I thought the whole thing had sounded too good to be true. Here we are in a new country for the first time and we get invited to hang out with some hot girl and her friends? Yeah, right. Maybe we were both hallucinating and the conversation never took place.

But when I quickly texted back that it was Nick and Mark from the plane, I got a completely different response. It turns out she didn't recognize the number or the name on the incoming text as it was on a corporate account

When she realized it was Nick and me she told us to come to a place called Bar 97 and ask for the Linh table. We jumped in a taxi a few minutes later and headed over to what turned out to be not a typical bar, but a club.

The music was pounding and I immediately knew that I would be suffering some permanent hearing damage as a result of this visit. The volume was so loud that you couldn't hear or be heard even if you were shouting into someone's ear.

It didn't much matter as the twenty or so people around the table simply smiled, danced in place and kept their drinks full. There were almost too many bottles of liquor to count, and glasses full of ice and booze. Before I even mouthed a hello to our host, a team of waiters got to work and handed me a glass with ice while one of the guests started pouring alcohol. A moment later a half dozen glasses came toward me and I heard a shout that turned out to be "Can ly," a Vietnamese term for "Cheers!"

The toasts continued nonstop for the next hour and a half because you never went more than a few minutes without a "Can ly" and a sip of your drink. It all made me smile. All I could think was that these people sure know how to have a good time. Both Nick and I seemed to be the only outsiders in the group, and I stood out in the club as the only Caucasian. I also stood a good head taller than many of the revelers as I'm just a shade less than six feet two inches tall. It didn't matter that I looked different or couldn't speak the language; I was welcomed like an old friend on a night where it felt like the party would never end.

Wrecked But Not Wrecked

At around 11:30 the group started to move out, but the night was hardly over. My Linh told us they were heading to another place and we were invited to come along. I guess we had definitely made a new set of friends even though we had barely spoken a word, confirming once again that booze and music can make some magic in the right environment. This was definitely turning into one of the best on-location experiences we had ever had and it was still our first day!

The group was heading down the stairs and out the front door to grab cars, scooters, taxis or whatever else they drove in this town. While trying to clear my ears and regain some hearing I picked up on the fact that they were waiting for a single car to be brought over by the valet. There had to be a dozen people standing there, not including Nick and me, so I asked for the name of the next spot and said we'd grab a taxi and meet them. *Fugettaboutit*, as they say in Staten Island. They weren't hearing any of it. We were going with the gang. *How would that be possible with all of these people,* I wondered. *Had they rented a bus?*

No such luck, it turns out. I realized that the evening was going to get even more interesting when a Chevrolet Equinox with seating for seven rolled up. Seeing that we couldn't all possibly fit I mentioned again that we'd be happy to grab a taxi and even take a couple of them with us in it. That was my second strike as they insisted on all of us going together. I soon found myself in the front passenger seat acting as a chair to two young Vietnamese women I hadn't met until that day. Things could certainly be worse, I thought. This wasn't so bad, at least for me.

When I turned to check on Nick I saw a single Taiwanese in a sea of Vietnamese faces somewhere between the car's second and third row. Nick's bemused expression told me that he was hammered, although I wasn't far behind him. I thought, what a crazy night! I go from watching fall lacrosse games to drinking with strangers half a world away in the blink of an eye.

The driver slipped into her seat next to me and at that moment my concern shot up. As it turns out, she was the actual birthday girl of the evening, and she was feeling no pain. As we started to pull away from the curb she balanced a phone in one hand and held the steering wheel in the other. What would my mother think? She would tell me I was a "jackass."

Now you have to understand what it's like to drive in Vietnam, especially in Ho Chi Minh, its largest city. The word that keeps coming to mind is chaos. There are seven million people here and almost as many scooters. Indeed, the scooter or motorbike count comes in at roughly five million, and they are everywhere.

You won't see lanes marked with the traditional yellow or white lines. In fact, on many of these streets, you won't see any lane markings at all. Lights? Forget about those too. They exist, but you wouldn't know it as we rolled along. What we did see was the flow of traffic like some kind of snake weaving in and out of the streets of the city. It was like it was alive and seeking something that it could never find as it never stopped moving.

Even though it's chaotic, it somehow seems to work. People were getting from one place to the next and we didn't witness a single wreck.

I wish I could say that for our driver, but alas, she was a wreck. The birthday girl had had more than her fair share of alcohol. I could probably say the same thing about everyone jammed into the car—more than a dozen of us—as we left the relative safety of a side street and ventured into the congested main arteries. The only thing that made me feel a bit of comfort was the fact that traffic here moved at a very slow pace. Even in the case of an unfortunate accident, the result would simply be what we call a fender bender.

As we headed down the road I learned something new about driving in Vietnam; in order to make a left turn you simply made your way into the left lane of the entire road. Don't worry if that lane is filled with oncoming traffic as indeed it is. Just start snaking your way over to the left curb and eventually you'll be able to make that left turn. The cars in your way will have to decide which side they will choose, but choose they will. Interesting barely describes the experience.

Craziness at Apocalypse Now

We finally rolled to a safe stop in front of a place called Apocalypse Now. Talk about a surreal name for a bar in Vietnam, given the movie by that title! A mix of foreigners and locals were divided into several areas, including a dance section, a stand-up bar and a spot with tables and chairs. Someone in our group must have been a regular as we were whisked to a table near the dance floor where a bottle of Grey Goose appeared alongside some Orangina. Shouts of "Can ly" began again in earnest as the party continued into the wee hours.

As we moved to the music and worked on the bottle of Goose another situation started to develop. It was like one of the storms you see in the Midwest where a funnel cloud takes shape, only to touch down and wreak havoc. Right before my eyes I watched two of the girls in our group go from dancing in place to dancing with each other. They ran their hands up and down each other's bodies as if they were lovers, feeling every curve and indentation. They moved fluidly with the beat of the music and I was mesmerized. It was like watching every man's fantasy, or at least the fantasy of most of the men I know, unfold before your eyes. I'm sure I had that deer-in-the-headlights look, if someone had bothered to even notice I was standing there. It didn't matter because the only thing anybody in viewing distance was looking at were these beautiful women and the display they were putting on.

Had anyone even noticed me they might have come to the conclusion that I was on some type of anti-psychotic medication, given away by my expression. It could have resembled one or more of the patients in the classic movie *One Flew Over the Cuckoo's Nest.*

What happened next dropped me down from a standing trance to the closest stool against the wall five feet behind me. One woman turned her back toward the other and as the woman behind caressed her breasts, the woman in front moved her hips like a jackhammer against her friend's pelvis.

"That's it, I'm done!" I thought as Nick turned looking for me. What was taking place had the same effect on him and we were both experiencing what some might call shock and awe.

Because I had mysteriously dropped out of sight, I waved my arm so he could see where I was. He made his way over to me, weaving slightly. "Dude, did you see that?" I asked. Nick replied with "Holy shit." I said, "That's ridiculous, we need to go." At the rate this was going, we'd be here till the sun came up and maybe even get ourselves into some unwanted trouble.

More importantly, it was approaching 3:00 in the morning and we had to leave the hotel by 9:00 a.m. to join the boat. A couple of hours of sleep was better than nothing, so off we went.

So ultimately, I did dodge a bullet of sorts, and later, alone in my hotel room, you could say that I still was feeling the shock and awe as I gingerly moved my woozy, pounding head from one side of the pillow to another. As I drifted into a fitful sleep, all I could really think of was *What would Ho Chi Minh have said about this?*

6

Murphy's International Fitness Plan

Have you ever tried to stay in shape when you travel? It's really, really hard. When you're constantly globe-hopping like me, your food choices can be as limited as your time, making it difficult to make the right choice on many occasions. Add to this the challenge of finding a gym in some countries and you'll understand why it's easy to gain five, ten or even fifteen pounds on a single trip.

The cruise industry in particular makes it very difficult as they make it easy to constantly eat, whether you're hungry or not. They have the normal dining options, the buffets that always seem to be open, the soft-serve ice cream by the pool, the unlimited soda passes, and more. What's a traveler to do?

It's really quite simple. You need to recognize your challenges, employ some creative ways to exercise and, most importantly, find some really vile food to sample, which of course could make you lose some unwanted travel weight in a hurry.

Believe me, I know all about this topic. Allow me to share my own professionally road-tested regimen for staying fit and keeping those pounds off.

Recognize the Temptation

The idea is to stay disciplined and stick to your goals, but all too often that fleeting thought quickly goes out the window due to a single phrase: "I'm on vacation!"

That simple statement gives most people a mental pass to stuff their faces with anything and everything, all in the name of their holiday. I have to admit that I've succumbed to this mindset on a number of occasions, especially on cruises.

One particular line that I sail on regularly is SeaDream Yacht Club. The challenge I have with them involves one of their handmade desserts that I drool about when I think of it...just as I'm doing right now as I slobber all over my keyboard!

That dessert is a molten chocolate concoction that will make even the last person to eat dessert, typically me, a raving lunatic at the end of dinner. Not only do I look forward to the night when they are going to serve it, I've taken things a step further by asking them to prepare it for me every night. So trust me when I tell you that I understand your pain and challenge when trying to remain disciplined on vacation. You can try really hard and still end up looking like the bastard child of Mama Cass Elliot and Orson Wells.

But just like saying "I'm Mark, and I'm a molten chocolate addict" in some warped twelve-step support group, recognizing your weaknesses is actually the first step on your road to healthful fitness. Hey, it works for me. Now please pass my SeaDream dessert.

Deal with the Frustration

At least when I'm onboard SeaDream I can use their small gym to get my workout completed. It doesn't stop me from gaining those ten or even fifteen pounds, but it certainly makes the number lower than it would have been. Try doing that in other places and you'll understand the challenge.

For example, on a recent trip to Spain I couldn't find any centrally located hotel in Seville that had a gym. My travel agent tried all of the four-star and five-star hotels, and not one of them had an actual fitness center. How are you expected to stay in shape when you travel if you can't even get some quick cardio or weight training in? I know I can't because I tend to eat too much bread and drink too much wine when traveling, especially in such a foodie paradise like Spain.

For the places that do have fitness centers, especially in Europe and the Middle East, their schedules will boggle the mind. I've stayed in hotels where the gym doesn't open until 10:00 a.m. and closes promptly at 5:00 p.m. That means you can't work out before you go out for the day, and by the time you return, it's closed yet again. Are these things for show or am I missing something here? If they are only going to be open when people aren't there, then tell me what exactly is the point?

Embrace the Dedication

I could go on and on about not being able to work out, or I can share some ideas on how you can maintain your exercise routine even if you don't have access to a gym when you travel. One way is to carry exercise bands that have handles on each end. You can buy them in different resistance levels and they are easy to pack. Exercise bands are great for a variety of strength-training moves and take up little to no space in your luggage.

Another item I like to bring along is known as the Perfect Pushup, a compact set of handles that dramatically increase the results you get versus doing standard pushups. They were designed by ex-Navy Seals—guys who know a thing or two about training. The Perfect Pushup is also easily packed. These devices take up very little space and guarantee you the opportunity to get in that important strength-training even when no gym is available. Just make sure you buy the travel version as they fold up flat and can fit in a side pocket of your luggage.

It's not all about working out, though. The real trick to staying in shape on the road doesn't come down to exercise; it comes down to diet. Indeed, personal trainers will tell you that staying in shape comes down to eighty-five percent diet and fifteen percent exercise.

Exercise is important for many reasons, but it's not a cure-all. That's why you'll see plenty of people who seem to exercise endlessly yet never make an impact on their appearance. They don't take care of the first part, which relates to proper diet. A workout gives them "permission" to eat and drink even more.

If you truly hate to exercise or do anything physical, simply take a walk for thirty minutes or more each day. This will help your overall well-being and can be coupled with the right diet. This is easy to do when you travel, as you'll probably have plenty of opportunities to walk and explore different sites and cities.

If you think the word "diet" means not eating you need not worry. You can eat! It's more about making the right choices of *what* to eat, and there really is no limit to those. Order the grilled chicken with steamed vegetables instead of the chicken parmigianino smothered in cheese. Order a special meal for your long flights, or follow my lead and carry on your own food and water so you aren't tempted to try unhealthy snacks or the fat-loaded meals that are so prevalent on board.

This is about dedication to your fitness. C'mon now...I know you can do it!

Consume Fresh Fish

You also can make sure that you eat plenty of fresh—and I mean *really fresh*—fish, which is known to be high in valuable omega-3 fatty acids. That's what I apparently did on a trip to Cambodia.

I was traveling by riverboat on a brand-new vessel known as the *La Marguerite*, operated by a company called AMAWaterways. The ship was built in Vietnam for foreign travelers who want to see that country. The rich dark woods and high-end detailing meshed very well with the romanticized feel of the destination, not necessarily how the local population lives. For that you might want to try a stay in one of the local villages we stopped in along our seven-night river journey.

The owners of the boat had a group come on board to experience the ship for the first time and we sailed from Ho Chi Minh City in Vietnam all the way down the Mekong to Siem Reap. Each day we would stop in different villages to experience life there. On some stops we'd check out a small silk factory while in others we might see how reed mats are made by hand.

In one place we checked out a floating village. Most families there lived in what were essentially three-room houses that sat on pontoons and remained tethered to other houses that were similarly placed. Many had a trap door in the center of the main house that was flipped open to feed the fish that lived beneath it. These were no ordinary houses, but instead actual fish farms. The fish would go crazy as food was dropped in. This was good because they were being raised for food themselves, and would be sold off and eventually placed on dinner plates all over Asia.

The fish farm we visited was a house that ran about twenty feet in one direction and thirty feet in another—basically a floating rectangle. The largest part of the house was the spot over the fish and where the trap door was located. The bathroom and living quarters represented the rest of the house, which amounted to roughly half of the overall home. Which got me thinking.

All around the work area of the house were mounds of what looked like scat, emitting an odor that would bring you to the verge of retching (which in itself can be a very effective regimen to keep those pounds off). These mounds were the ground-up remains of fish parts that would be turned into smaller pellets and fed to their unsuspecting finned cousins swimming beneath the house.

As I stood there taking in this setup, I thought about how lucky most of us are to live the way we do. Has one of your kids ever done a sleepover at your neighbors' floating fish farm and scat shack? I think not. And how about personal hygiene? Given the size of the overall house, and its proximity to the fish underneath, where in the world does the bathroom fit in? Better yet, where's the plumbing? Is the Mekong simply the largest toilet in the country? I couldn't tell you unless I donned some scuba gear and went beneath the house for a visual inspection. That was not going to happen anytime soon, so I was left to wonder. These are not ideal living conditions, but certainly are common in this part of the world. Once again, I thank God for being born where I was and the inherent advantages that provided.

I saw a number of these floating fish farms where families are making a living raising and selling fish from right beneath their floor. I wouldn't be surprised if I had some fish from one of these farms during my stay here or in other parts of Asia, as these floating villages are big producers for the region. It made me think of that saying, "You are what you eat," but with a twist. What if you are what the fish you just ate, ate? On second thought, let's not go there.

...or, Just Eat Some Duck Embryo

Ultimately, staying fit and keeping those pounds off while traveling involved, for me at least, a moment of courage at the prodding of my producer Nick to do something a bit different for one of our segments. What Nick was hoping I'd do is try a common Vietnamese street food known as *balut* and discuss the experience on camera. If you never heard of balut you probably aren't alone. I'd never heard of it either until this trip even though it is very common and eaten by the locals here as part of their core diet.

Balut is a baby duck embryo that is just over twenty weeks old and in the shell. It is prepared by steaming the egg and then sold in quantities of five for a dollar. Locals eat it because they say it tastes good (not) and it provides some cheap protein for their diet. I ate it to create some shock value for the video we were shooting. As it turns out, it was a shock to me as well, and most definitely resulted in some rapid weight loss.

The way you eat these eggs is pretty straightforward. Crack off the top of the shell, but *don't look down into it!* That was the warning I received from pretty much everyone who had gathered around to see me attempt this. *"Don't look!"*

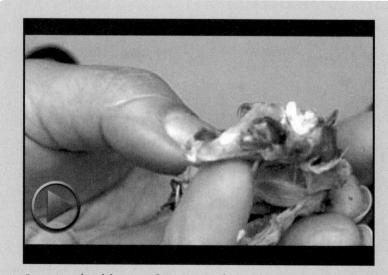

Staring at this delicacy makes me soooo hungry!

After you remove the top, add some salt and pepper to the egg and raise it to your mouth. The lady who was my personal balut trainer was guiding me every step of the way, with her first instruction being to "suck the juice." Their version of "juice" is really just the fluid that the duck embryo was in before it got nice and hot from being steamed.

So is it okay to call it "embryo juice"? I guess it is okay to call it that as well as drink it. I can't say I recall the taste too well as my hand was shaking as I raised the shell up to my lips.

After accomplishing this little feat my next step was to eat the embryo itself. As I started to dig in I was stopped by one of the observers who informed me that I needed to add some salt and pepper, along with lemon juice, and a mint leaf, all designed to eliminate the "fishy" smell. *What am I doing* I thought as I processed that statement. *Fishy smell? Why does a duck smell "fishy"...oh, never mind.*

How's it sounding so far? Are you hungry yet? I wasn't, but with the camera rolling and the gathering crowd of fellow travelers and locals urging me on with high amusement, there was no stopping at this point. With everything all set I couldn't delay any further. I dug in and scooped the duck into my mouth. I chewed it up and then took a big swallow and it was finally over.

My "helper" said "yummy," but I beg to differ. You might be asking yourself *How did it taste?* Honestly, I'm not sure I can even remember what it actually tasted like. I do know one thing; it wasn't good.

After I did my little tasting they pulled the body of one of the duck embryos out of another shell to show me the beak, eyes and even the feathers that were developing. *Don't look?* Well, at least I didn't have to see what I was eating until after the fact. I probably wouldn't have been able to get it down if I had!

I felt like I was part of the home team now that I had experienced this dish firsthand. I was excited to share my experience with some of the locals we had met that first night in Vietnam, a group that we would reconnect with on our final two nights in the country. It was a low-key affair as we hung out in a lounge versus a club and I shared my experiences over the past seven nights. I was like a kid with a secret from the moment that I sat down. I was simply dying to tell them all that I had tried balut! Our host from the first night, My Linh, just looked at me with a funny smile when I told her what I had consumed.

"Really, you ate the whole thing?" she asked.

"Yes, isn't that cool?" I responded with an ear-splitting grin. I was really proud of my little mind-over-matter accomplishment!

"I won't eat it, the duck itself that is. I'll only eat the little egg yolk that's inside of it."

"You don't eat balut?" I practically shouted out. Perhaps the local beer was having an effect.

"No way," she responded, making a slight face that seemed to be halfway between disgust and amused mockery.

What the heck? Not everyone spoke English and didn't know what we were talking about, so I asked her about her friends and whether they ate it. Each and every one of them shook their heads from side to side as they smiled at me. Not a single one in this group actually ate these things.

Throughout the evening we ran into more and more people who were told of my little accomplishment through our translator. I couldn't understand what they were saying, but the response was almost universal. Their noses would twist up a little as they displayed that same slight look of disgust coupled with bemusement.

My Vietnamese bonding moment was passing with no bond whatsoever. As it turned out, of the twenty or so different people who eventually showed up, and who all lived there, not one of them actually eats that "local" food. At that point I felt like I needed to check the restroom mirror to see if "SILLY TRAVEL CORRESPONDENT" was stamped on my forehead.

And Now for the Weight Loss Part

The next day I started to understand a potential reason for the underwhelming reaction my culinary feat received. I was eating a late breakfast outside the hotel at a local Pho restaurant. If you haven't tried Pho, you should. This traditional Vietnamese dish is one part soup, one part noodle, one part vegetable and one part beef, shrimp, chicken or seafood. It's very tasty and low in fat too.

As I was enjoying this meal I had a sudden rumble from my stomach. It struck immediately and wasn't going to go away. I needed a bathroom and I needed one immediately! I asked at the counter by doing my best mime imitation. (Imagine that, if you will, but don't think about it for too long. It wasn't pretty!) The worker pointed out the back door at another door with a sign on the other side of a small ally and I headed toward it, not without a little dread.

It's bad enough using a public restroom in your home country. It gets beyond interesting in some of the places where I've traveled. If I could have, um…*held it* I would have, but I really didn't have a choice at that point.

Thankfully, the bathroom turned out to be quite nice and I was able to handle my immediate problem. I returned to the restaurant and felt absolutely fine. I was relieved in more ways than one, as I took it to mean I wasn't getting sick, just experiencing a little bit of discomfort. That relief wouldn't last, as I had similar experiences off and on over the next few days. In fact, the symptoms continued even after my return to the States.

It was possible that I had picked up some kind of bug in Vietnam or Cambodia, maybe even from that little duck embryo. It's not something you want to take lightly so I headed off to the doctor, even though I felt completely fine most of the time. It seemed to hit me only when I ate something, but hit me it did.

The doctor wouldn't prescribe any kind of antibiotics, as he's a bit neurotic about them. He insisted that we first have to determine what kind of intelligent life, if any, might be making a home inside me. First thing he needed to do was run some tests, but it would take up to a week to learn the results. *Ugh,* I thought. *A week? What should I do in the meantime if this continues?* His answer: "Go on a liquid diet for three days, eating only clear fluids, broths, and the like."

Ugh, again. At this point I'd gone from a weight of 185 pounds before my trip to 178 just before my new "diet." Three days later I weighed in at 170, a number I hadn't seen since college. The idea behind the liquid diet is to starve the little critters that are causing the havoc and basically kill them. The effect on me was to drop my weight to a point that hadn't been seen in more than two decades.

Beautiful, Fit Me

As it turns out, there were no little critters, just a bit of gastrointestinal distress that eventually went away. It's hard to put my finger on any one thing I ate, but my money is on that poor little unhatched duck eaten on a muddy riverbank in Cambodia.

My knees and back are quite thankful to that little feathered delicacy, as the loss of an extra twenty pounds has done wonders for them as well as for my overall energy level. It made me realize that time adds pounds and pressure on your body that you don't really notice until it's gone. It also gave me the motivation to take the whole trend one step further.

To get myself to what I weighed during my days of playing college basketball I had to kick my workouts up a notch and get as tight as I've ever been. I had a trip to Israel that was coming up in June, about nine months after my Vietnam experience, so I made this my goal. It was something to shoot for as I'd be floating in the Dead Sea and doing mud treatments, giving me a strong incentive

Eat some funky food and stay in shape!

to try and look my best. I didn't quite reach my ultimate goal of six-pack abs, but I certainly was happy with the result.

So what's the moral of this story? You could eat some funky food, catch a bug, and maybe lose some weight. That works...but you have easier ways to get there that are just as effective.

7

The Santorini Shakedown

Any trip to Greece has to include its renowned and rugged islands. One of the most spectacular of these is Santorini, an old volcanic caldera set in the Aegean Sea, about 200 kilometers (120 miles) southeast of the Greek mainland. This little piece of paradise is known for its incredible views, ancient history and maze of whitewashed houses connected like a big jigsaw puzzle.

Most people visit Santorini the way we did, via a cruise that spends up to a day anchored in the small harbor between the uninhabited volcanic islet of Nea Kameni and the village of Fira. Tenders from the anchored ships then transport visitors back and forth to the dock at the base of the cliff that soars 400 meters (more than 1,300 feet) straight up to Fira. Tourists can climb on a path that winds its way up, ride donkeys on that same path or jump on the high-speed cable car.

We took the cable car, at least on the way up. Our trip down was a bit more interesting, and time-consuming, but not by choice. It seems that the good folks in these parts have a proprietary view of their donkey paths, especially after night has fallen.

In Fira, it's impressive how the whitewashed houses interconnect with one another. One person's roof is another's terrace in this most unusual and unique destination. We decided to explore this maze just beyond the shopping area packed with vendors and storefronts offering local merchandise and crafts. We wandered down paths that twisted and turned, not sure where one house began and the other ended. It was fascinating indeed.

We ultimately found ourselves at a small restaurant and bar that made a great location to watch the sunset over Nea Kameni. We set up our cameras, shot our wrap, and then let the camera run to capture the setting sun. We would then use that footage to show a time lapse version of the sunset to close out this particular segment.

We had some time on our hands until the sun disappeared, so we did what most people would do. Order a drink! The view was amazing. From this perch on high we were able to gaze far to sea, with unobstructed views of the sun setting in the distance. You could say "It doesn't get much better than this," and you'd be right in regard to the scenery. The only problem for me was that, despite being in this incredibly romantic setting, I was not with my wife, but with Nick, my multimedia producer. To make matters even worse, he barely said a word while we were partaking of our intimate little cocktail hour together.

Jeeze, I wasn't expecting that we would be cooing softly to one another about our dreams for the future, but at least we could have discussed the amazing experiences we were able to capture that day, or even current events or the ball scores

The views from Santorini are beguiling.

from home. Instead, Nick just played with his phone while occasionally making vaguely annoying slurping noises as he nursed his drink. How's that for the romantic life of the globe-hopping travel correspondent? Indeed, as I write this I've created a new nickname for my intrepid traveling companion; he is now to be known as No Talk Nick.

I tried to temper my regret of not being with a lovely female by quickly sucking down three mojitos. No Talk Nick matched me swig for swig, even though neither of us is particularly known for our ability to handle alcohol. And maybe that's why we were so nonchalant about the time passing as the evening's deadline approached for getting back down the hill to the tender that would take us back to the cruise ship.

Finally, after the sun's golden orb deliciously melted into the ocean, we finished the last of our drinks, packed up the equipment and made our way back toward the cable car.

Shakedown Showdown

The last tender to the cruise ship was leaving at 8:00 p.m. and it was now 7:30, so we strolled comfortably into the main area of town carrying both our equipment and a nice buzz. We had anticipated a wait of ten minutes or so and then a couple of minutes straight down the side of the cliff, leaving us plenty of time to spare. The fog of alcohol was quickly replaced when we saw an extensive line leading to the cable car. *Oh crap,* I thought, there's no way we can get on a cable car in enough time to make it down to the tender by 8:00 p.m. It would be the last run of the evening, so if we missed it we'd be sleeping in Santorini and figuring out how to catch up to the ship the next day. This wasn't anything I was interested in contemplating.

I turned to an official-looking person wearing a uniform who happened to work for one of the cruise lines that were in port that day. I asked her how long it would take to walk down the cliff to the dock because the cable car was out of the question. "Thirty minutes," she replied.

I looked at my watch and it was already passing 7:35. Panic started to set in. "Let's go!" I barked to Nick as we turned left and high-tailed it for the trail. Lights from restaurants and businesses illuminated the path running down the first few twists, but all too soon they were replaced with much darker stretches as we made our way further and further down from town.

As the path got darker we noticed something else: dark mounds that made walking treacherous. These weren't boulders or rocks that had rolled down, but donkey dung that had been dropped by those most industrious workers that had spent the daylight hours bringing tourists up and down the path. It seemed that every other step put you at risk of stepping in the dung, so we were on high alert.

As we made our way down the hill, a whole group of other people and their beasts of burden were heading up. The guys who handled the donkeys were done for the day and some of them were making their final trek to the top before calling it a night. They weren't doing anything for us, but that didn't stop each of them from demanding payment. I guess they felt that they owned this path. Donkey or no donkey, everyone had to pay, kind of like the New Jersey Turnpike.

Bullshit! I've spent too many years living in New York to have some donkey jockey shake me down. *I'm going to pay you so I can walk down the path, and maybe even step in a land mine on the way? Not going to happen, my friends, not going to happen,* I thought.

We rounded bend after bend, besieged by the never-ending demands for "payment." With one hand on a donkey lead and the other extended out in front of me, it was clear the shakedown was in full swing. As I struggled to maintain my balance and avoid the droppings, I made my view about this known in a rather vociferous manner. I'm not sure they would have agreed if they understood what I was saying.

"Sure, no problem. Let me give you my ATM card," or "Do you take Visa?" were just some of the responses they got from me while Nick cringed. I'm not shy about voicing my opinion and laughing about it at the same time. I know the donkey dudes didn't think it was funny as I blew right past them, but I was actually cracking myself up as I came up with more and more things to share along the way.

Poor Nick thought we might end up as donkey food...or worse. As strangers walking down a very dark path in a foreign country, perhaps we'd never be found or even identified! Maybe these rough-looking characters would simply knock us off, then unceremoniously cart our remains away on the swaying rumps of donkeys before happily feeding us to the Aegean fish while they smoked, swilled grassi and laughed about our foolishness!

"How about a check?" I continued, undeterred, as the donkey men glowered at me. "Better yet, how about some traveler's checks?"

"Visa! Everywhere you want to be." I was a walking, talking commercial for various payment systems, though I did fail to mention PayPal. With my smart-ass slap-downs I was even starting to annoy myself a little, but I was on a roll. This was just too much fun.

When I ran out of payment options I shifted to providing some more tactical advice. I suggested places they might look for the particular payment they were seeking. One of the suggestions being the ass of the donkeys they were taking up the hill. I figured they had about as much of a chance of getting a Euro or two out of me as they did of having their donkeys shit Euros. Forget the Golden Goose, just give me a donkey that craps Euros.

I was giving them a bit of their own medicine and, you might even say, a free consulting session. I provided some insights into how they could expand their base of future revenues but didn't even get a simple "thank you." Ingrates!

The Final Sprint

My running dialog stopped as the last of the donkey handlers passed by, and I knew that time was running out. I had to really kick it into gear to make it to the bottom and the tender that would take us to the ship.

With its engines running and its crew scanning for any last remaining passengers, namely us, we knew we had a fighting chance. And that's exactly when it happened. On the second to final turn I almost lost Nick as he haplessly skidded on a mountain of dung. He caught himself at the last second and avoided the humiliation of actually ending up butt-down in excreta. His shoes, however, weren't so lucky. Nick likes to buy sneakers, and fancy ones at that, that he keeps completely spotless.

"Aww shit," he said as he looked down at those designer sneakers. Indeed.

"Let's go!" I yelled from ahead and Nick half limped and ran trying to catch up.

We didn't have any time to spare so, dung and all, we made it the final few steps with Nick ditching his shoes before jumping on the tender and the ship that awaited us. We had a segment in hand, even though Nick at that point was barefoot.

Safely motoring back to the mother ship, the moist sea air blowing in my face, I suddenly felt a little giddy. It truly doesn't get much better than this, I thought, No Talk Nick notwithstanding. What's a little donkey dung or even a Santorini-style shakedown to cap off the experiences we enjoyed today? It's all sweet, and just another day in an unscripted life.

8

Israel and the Camel Guy

You never really know what's going to happen during a trip to Israel. One minute you're mesmerized by historical wonders, gazing upon ancient ruins revered for centuries by the millions of believers who flock to the Holy Land. The next you're marveling that literally everyone in the country seems to be at the pinnacle of technology. No surprise really, as this tiny country (it comprises roughly one-sixth of one percent of the entire Middle East Region) is second only to Silicon Valley in terms of high-tech firms and startups.

You'll find other contrasts, too. One minute you're being slathered with mud by a horny senior citizen, and the next you're preparing to dodge a projectile thrown by a nasty guy on a camel. Let me explain…

Sensual Sludge

On one recent trip to Israel my crew and I planned to traverse the country to capture some great Travel Unscripted footage. The basic plan was to start in Tel Aviv, the country's most modern city, and then make our way up the coast. We intended to explore Roman ruins, visit an Arab town, and hit the resorts along the Dead Sea.

The Dead Sea, despite possessing a name that is a public relations nightmare, is a unique body of water. It's really a salt lake, located about 1,400 feet below sea level and containing nearly nine times as much sodium as either the Atlantic or Pacific Oceans. On the downside, obviously, there's not much life in the Dead Sea. On the plus side, it's a difficult spot in which to drown. The extreme saline content creates buoyancy that allows even the most unskilled of swimmers to bob around like a beach ball in a hot tub. It's also known for its health resorts and abundant supply of greenish mud.

Mud is not usually considered a tourist attraction, but Dead Sea mud is so full of minerals, so conducive to healing, that visitors from around the world come here to wallow in it. In most locales mud is something to avoid, something that gets on your shoes and tracks up the carpet. At the Dead Sea it's a prized item, a literal fountain of goop. My crew and I had viewed plenty of shots featuring hot babes smearing themselves with this slime, and thus felt that filming such an auspicious sight would be appreciated by our viewers.

Upon arrival we discovered that the legendary hot babes had been replaced by a crowd of semi-elderly Israelis. The lack of mud-babes might have had something to do with the fact that there's no Dead Sea mud at the developed areas of the Dead Sea. You can't just reach down, grab a handful, and start smearing yourself. Instead, you must buy a bucket of mud from your resort, which gets the stuff from other parts of the sea that aren't accessible to tourists.

Can I sue for sexual harassment?

This is some high-dollar sludge, but because it seemed like it might make an interesting segment I bought a bucket and headed to the beach. The crew set up the cameras (still no hot babes in sight) and I prepared to deliver some background for the viewers. One old gal seemed curious about our show, and I recruited her to hold my mud bucket. I explained that I would emerge from the sea, walk toward the camera, reach into the bucket, and slap some mud on my chest.

All was going as planned until I reached for a fistful of premium ooze. This seventy-year-old woman had different plans; she appointed herself my own personal body-painter. It would have been nice if she'd been forty years younger, but that's the risk you take when you film unscripted. She slathered me up, down and sideways, made it into our segment, threw me a wink and strolled off into the sunset.

I've a feeling that all the old girl's friends have now heard the story of how she seduced a crazy American with nothing more than her feminine wiles and a bucket of semi-indigenous muck. The gossip hotline at her temple must be working overtime.

Mountains and Desert with a Space Oddity

Our next stop on this whirlwind tour of Israel was the legendary mountain fortress known as Masada. According to the most reputable histories, King Herod fortified this massive, flat-topped mountain between 37 and 31 B.C. After his death it was appropriated by the Roman Empire.

A sect of Jews, who were not exactly thrilled with the idea of becoming Roman slaves (or being killed), defeated the Roman garrison stationed at Masada in 66 A.D. Six years later the Romans, always a bit possessive of their real estate, decided to take it back. This was no small feat. Masada's vertical cliffs are nearly 1,400 feet high on one side and 300 feet high on the

Exploring the lunar landscape near the Dead Sea.

other. Furthermore, Herod had outfitted the joint with twelve-foot-high walls, towers, storehouses for food, an armory, barracks, and deep cisterns of water. It was the sort of place where a small band could hold off a large army almost indefinitely.

Which is exactly what happened.

The Romans surrounded Masada with 15,000 troops, and eventually built an earthen ramp up the mountain's shorter side. A battering ram was set at the end of the ramp, and finally the walls of Masada were breached. The legions poured in, but instead of finding the resilient fighters who had kept them at bay for so long, they were met with an eerie silence. The small group of Jews (estimated to be between 700 and 900 men, women, and children) who had held Masada for so long and under such adverse conditions, had chosen suicide over slavery. Only two women and several children were found alive.

The top of Masada is now reached by either an incredibly strenuous hour-long walk, or a gondola ride that takes minutes. We chose the latter. That was partly because we were hauling equipment, partly due to time constraints, and partly because my producer, Nick, smokes like a chimney (though he vehemently denies this indisputable fact at every opportunity).

The next day we ventured south of the resort areas and into the barren desert. Our guide was a fellow name Gil, a Jeep-driving maniac with a talent for hitting every gully, bump, obstruction and bone-dry gorge in the most barren areas of the Israeli outback. During this kidney-killer of a ride we were treated—over and over—to Gil's favorite song. He seemed to have a thing for David Bowie's "Space Oddity."

This was okay, at first, because "Space Oddity" is also one of my favorite songs. I even asked to have it played back a couple of times, as it put us in this otherworldly state as we crested a hill that could have been on the moon. But after a few back-to-back repetitions, however, it might have slipped out of my personal Top Forty. I made myself a promise to send Gil some new CDs once we returned to civilization. Maybe some Rolling Stones, maybe some Sinatra...maybe even the Alvin and the Chipmunks Christmas album.

We hadn't planned a Jeep trip through the desert, but it was worth it. The views ranged from alien moonscapes to breathtaking panoramas of swirling sand to distant views of the Dead Sea. In a word, it was totally unplanned and utterly spectacular. We stood upon ground that had remained literally unchanged since others had trodden it thousands of years prior. We tasted the salt that made up the large hills. We felt the cooling aspects of the mini caves that appeared in the walls of the hills. We put our heads inside one of these caves and felt the temperature drop by more than twenty degrees, akin to walking into an air-conditioned house.

American Floookas and the Flying Shoe

Next up was Jerusalem, that crossroads of the world known for such sites as the Wailing Wall, the Dome of the Rock, the Mount of Olives and the most despicable and obnoxious purveyor of camel rides on the planet.

We'd spent a couple of days in Jerusalem, and as is fairly typical of Travel Unscripted, we planned to shoot the introduction last. We'd chosen the Mount of Olives primarily for its historical significance, but mostly because filming from that spot provided a fantastic view of the city below.

I'm not sure how or why we had been distracted, but we were near the end of our stay when we remembered that we'd not yet shot our intro. We hopped in our car, raced to the spot we'd earlier selected, and began setting up our equipment.

That's when we heard him. In fact, that's when all of Jerusalem heard him. The nastiest, dirtiest, most foul-mouthed camel owner in the entire Middle East was cursing a group of tourists and their guide. Although he seemed to speak some sort of Arab dialect, he had managed to expand his education to the point where he knew the word "Fuck." It' didn't quite come out right—it sounded more like "Floook"—but there was no mistaking the meaning.

The camel driver (let's just call him Ahab), via gibberish, hand gestures and his one mangled bit of western profanity, was telling the tourists to "floook this" and "floook that" and to "get the floook out of here."

This was a fluke occurrence, but it was the sort of flooking fluke that was going to ruin our shoot.

The tourists made a hasty exit, but Ahab continued his unending monologue to nobody in particular. I think he might have needed some anger management classes. I'm sure he needed a bath and a few thousand sticks of Right Guard. I felt sorry for the camel. The dude was wound tighter than an obsessive compulsive's clock spring. He was bipolar squared. If you curse out a group of tourists who don't take you up on your pitch, do you think the next group standing within earshot is going to think twice? Or simply ignore you?

We tried to ignore him, which of course was a physical impossibility. It would be like Bill Clinton trying to ignore a chubby intern, like Paris Hilton trying to ignore a diamond tennis bracelet for Chihuahuas, like John Travolta trying to ignore the fact that he starred in *Battlefield Earth*. We might as well have proclaimed that gravity was henceforth null and void. Quite simply, this spewing, vile, steaming pile of camel-toting pseudo-humanity was not about to pipe down or vacate the premises.

We only needed about thirty-five seconds of peace and quiet. If I nailed the intro on the first take we could have been out of there in fifteen. We thought that Ahab might tire himself out, or at least need to catch a breath. There was a moment of silence, just a brief moment, and I began my spiel.

Ahab started up again. The crew could hear him through their headphones; our mics were picking up every word. I walked over to the crew after standing there and casting a sideways glance in this guy's direction.

The ensuing conversation went something like this.

Ahab: Floooka, floooka, floooka...yabba dabba doo...

Mark: Can you guys hear him or should we simply shoot it?

Nick: Uhhhh...not a good idea. You can definitely hear him. Let's see if he shuts up.

Ahab: Aaaghhh stupid...?

Nick: There he goes again...

There's a slight break and we jump at the chance as I quickly move into position.

Mark: Okay, now. Let me know when were rolling...

Mark: *(begins intro)* The best place to start a tour of Jerusalem is at the Mount of Olives. It gives you a complete perspective of where you're going to be going and where you are.

Ahab: Googly ooogly…*and other unintelligible mutterings spew forth.*

Mark: Oh my God…this guy won't shut up. *(I turn in his direction)*…Hey, can you cut us a break over here?

Ahab: You go!

Mark: We're trying to work here…

Ahab: No flooka work here…

Mark: Nick, I'm about to tell this guy what he can do with that camel…

Nick: Uh, not a great idea…

Ahab: Yagga fooga doodah…

We held our breaths, so to speak.

Ahab: Floook wah diddie, diddie da, diddie do.

Mark: Hey dude, can you give me one minute so I can do this?

More muttering continued as the man finally made his way down the road and away from our location. I did some muttering of my own as I cursed this camel guy and our delay in getting this final bit of footage to wrap our entire trip. It finally came though, as we took care of the shot, packed our bags up, and closed out another Travel Unscripted journey.

9

Target Practice in Taiwan

I was excited about my first trip to Taiwan for a number of reasons, not the least of which is my love of Asian food. My producer, a Taiwanese native, claimed I would be even more enamored once we landed in Taipei. His descriptions of Taiwanese cuisine were full of epicurean promise, especially his tales regarding a particularly famous dim sum restaurant that was hardly ever raided by the local health department.

But, I'm getting ahead of myself. A well-worn Chinese proverb states that the journey of a thousand miles begins with a single step. That needs to be updated for the twenty-first century. Upon landing in Taipei we learned that the journey of a thousand miles begins with a single step whose direction has been fully studied, discussed, approved and sanitized for your protection by the official Taiwanese Department of Tourism. I was less than thrilled with the prospect. Filming our show as we do—on location in an unscripted manner—does not mesh well with rules, regulations and preplanned visits to locales and events deemed appropriate by the powers that be. Still, delusional though it might have been, I had hopes we could accomplish our goal.

In retrospect, I couldn't have been more wrong.

As soon as our plane touched down an emissary of the tourism department came to meet us. We were happily welcomed, happily packed into a minivan and happily whisked off to our hotel. It was all very happy, and the sheer volume of perpetual smiles reminded me of the Monty Python exhibit at Madame Tussaud's Wax Museum. We were provided with an itinerary, a timetable, suggested photo ops and convenient story suggestions. It was riveting stuff, which I promptly stuffed in my bag just in case our lodgings experienced a toilet paper shortage. Upon reaching the hotel we hurried to our rooms, showered, grabbed a bite to eat and were hustled back into the minivan for our first day of government-sanctioned exploration.

Tourism boards often organize this type of junket in order to showcase a destination's highlights, avoid its lowlights and receive as much free publicity as possible. Such trips tend to be tightly scheduled, cramming as many sights as possible into a very short window of time. We had been promised that we would be shown the most unique sights in all of Taiwan. I hoped that "unique" would not be defined as a tour of the post office.

We should have been so lucky. Our first stop was the hospital.

Medical Drama and the Soup Bath

Nothing immerses you in the ways and thoughts of a culture like the sight of doctors, nurses and hobbling patients garbed in peek-a-boo paper robes. Hell, we could have been in Toledo or Cleveland. It wasn't even an old hospital with historical significance; the facility was all glass and tasteful décor with nary a hint of indigenous pride. There were no warning signs informing us that our international health insurance did not cover procedures involving totemism or snake worship. The lobby did not include a large tank displaying Chiang Kai-shek's appendix.

For a moment I was glad I was in a top-notch medical facility. I was in the midst of a major WTF moment and felt that I might require a handful or six of powerful mood enhancers. At first glance there was nothing Taiwanese about this Taiwanese hospital, and I half expected to see Marcus Welby handing out corn-fed wisdom and sugar-free lollipops. Nobody, with the exclusion of people who have been bitten, stung, drowned, shot or hit by a bus, makes the hospital their number-one spot for vacational hijinks.

Our guide, her smile still plastered wide, apparently read the look of disappointment on my face. She rushed over, brimming with enthusiasm, and explained that this hospital had a department completely devoted to traditional Chinese medicine. The holistic methods employed would be something of which we were completely unaware in America. It would be something new and unique, she told me, something we had never experienced. The docs would check our energy (our "chi"), deliver therapeutic massages, provide healing herbal teas and tinctures and cure us of any maladies that might be present.

In other words, we were about to get probed.

Everyone in our group was pawed at by a Chinese physician, given a diagnosis and then prescribed a specific treatment. After a few minutes of hand waving, grunts and orders, things I couldn't understand at all, my interpreter told me that I had been diagnosed with "very high chi." I figured this was a good thing, signifying that my metaphorical cup was running over with energy.

Such was not the case. Apparently "chi" is roughly equivalent to oil pressure in a car. "Very high chi" is just as bad as "very low chi." My prescription was to sit for forty-five minutes in what I think could possibly have been a tub of beef broth. I'm not that fond of soaking, and thus lasted about fifteen minutes before I hopped out and toweled off. The doctor wasn't pleased—this might indicate that he has "very high chi" as well—but he went ahead and sent me off for the second part of my rehabilitative therapy. This turned out to be a massage, something I can enjoy for perpetuity. A quarter-hour of bathing in consommé is a small price to pay for a good massage. Things could have been much worse.

My main concern was the fact that we weren't accomplishing any actual work. I came to Taiwan to capture the essence of the destination and its various experiences, not to jump in a hot-tub full of bouillon cubes. However, the massage was giving me a false sense of security. Why not relax and go with the flow? I decided we could start filming at the next stop.

Once again, I decided wrong.

The Ancient Relics of Taiwan

Relaxed from massage, and smelling a bit like yesterday's soup, the crew and I were once again herded into the van. I expected our second stop to be a temple, maybe an obligatory tour of Taipei or a historical monument. After our stop at the shiny new hospital, I assumed our tour guide would want to show us some ancient relics.

She did. We went to a nursing home.

I still have no idea what sort of thought process was involved in picking such a destination. I don't why we were there or how a retirement center was supposed to further our appreciation of

Taiwanese culture. The age range of the residents was some-where between elderly and drooling. The coolest thing we saw, aside from wheelchairs and senility, was some guy riding around on a floor-polishing machine. It looked like a mini-Zamboni, which is highly appropriate because lightning-slick floors are just what you want in a facility where upwards of ninety percent of the residents are on canes or walkers.

We were led into a dining room, skating behind the Zamboni, and motioned to a couple of round tables. Instead of having lunch at a famous Taipei restaurant we would be dining in the nursing home's communal cafeteria. I suspect this was a cost-cutting measure. Visiting dignitaries receive the star treatment; travel writers are fed pureed carrots. Oddly, even though it was right around noon, the place was empty. Maybe the residents decided to hit the Early Bird Special, or maybe they were all on IVs.

Lunch was edible, which mostly proves that it's hard to screw up noodles. Moreover, when you're dining in a nursing home cafeteria your anticipatory bar is set fairly low.

We finished our meal and were ushered toward the exit. On the way out the nursing home staff loaded us down with brochures that presumably touted the features and amenities of the facility. It was a little like getting suckered into one of those "free" time-share visits where you suffer through an interminable sales pitch in order to get a complimentary night's stay and tickets to a John Denver tribute band. The brochures were written in Mandarin, which none of us could read, so I'll never know if I missed out on spending my twilight years in a Taipei old folk's home renowned for its somewhat digestible noodles and heavily accented rendi-tions of "Rocky Mountain High."

Chicken Ass and Other Delights

Our first day in Taipei had consisted of viewing sick folks and old folks. Upon returning to our hotel, my cameraman, Nick Choo, and I decided to sneak away from the watchful eyes of our well-meaning handlers and visit the Shih Lin Night Market. This is the real Taipei, a collection of 539 stalls operated primarily by ancient and inscrutable food vendors who last washed their hands in 1964. The Shih Lin Night Market gave me a new appreciation for even the most run-down and hygienically incorrect of dirty-water hot-dog carts in Manhattan. This was the real deal.

Most cultures pride themselves on the quality of their cuisine. Most cultures outside the United States also pride themselves on consuming every part of an animal, no matter how revolting. Not even the waste goes to waste. Hooves, tongues, brains, fins, guts, hide, eyeballs, antennae…if it can be fried, baked, boiled, slapped on a banana leaf or swallowed raw with incendi-

Chicken ass and pig's blood, anyone?

ary spices then somebody will eat it. This applies to beef, swine, bugs, reptiles, fish and fowl. I can say with first-hand certainty that most of the world's peoples eat every part of a chicken but the feathers and the beak…and I'm not all that certain the beak enjoys protected status.

You smell the Shih Lin market long before you see it. This is largely due to the popularity of "Stinky Tofu," the national dish of Taiwan. Imagine a hundred-yard line of port-a-johns at an outdoor rock concert. Imagine that the outhouses are parked next to a slaughterhouse adjoining a landfill…during August…in Death Valley. Stinky tofu aspires to have such a sweet aroma. The dish consists of a combination of fermented milk, fermented meat and some sort of unmentionable brine fermented inside a very old dog. Add dried shrimp, toss in the soybean curd and bury the mess in your backyard for at least six months. The good news is that you'll never have to mow the yard again. The bad news is that you might be fined for harboring an unregistered Superfund site.

Nick convinced me to try a bite. My advice is that you order your festering tofu fried, and cover it in hot sauce. Try not to breathe while you're chewing.

The gastronomic delights of Shih Lin were endless. Next up was pig's blood in pig's intestine stew. This is the type of dish that would have made Julia Child hang herself. The blood isn't dissolved in the broth; that would be way too easy. It floats around in jellied slices, similar in appearance to the very cheapest version of canned cranberry sauce. The intestines were edible, and really were no worse in taste and texture than a rubber band. If pork is "the other white meat," then pork intestines with hog's blood might be "the other white-trash meat."

The best was yet to come. People who make fun of Chicken McNuggets have never had the pleasure of chowing down on chicken ass. This is one of the specialties of the Shih Lin... the asshole of a chicken skewered on a stick and grilled over an open flame. Nick had told me about this, and I assumed he was just making it up. He wasn't. Chicken-ass kabobs are much loved all over Taipei. They have a slightly crunchy texture—it's all that health-giving cartilage—and come four or five to a stick. You really wouldn't know you were eating the ass of chicken unless you looked closely and noticed the little tiny sphincter. Not surprisingly, chicken ass tastes kind of like chicken.

That said, I don't think that Kentucky Fried Chicken-ass franchises will start popping up in the states anytime soon. I'm not saying that they won't—we did invent the corn dog—but I couldn't ever see such an entrée being as popular in New Jersey as it is in Taiwan. Those folks do chicken-ass right.

Staying Late at School

After half a bottle of Pepto Bismol and a good night's sleep I met the morning with a bit more hope. Upon leaving the hotel we headed off to Jiu Fen, a lovely mountaintop town about an hour outside of Taipei. It was raining like hell and we managed to shoot a bit of indoor video. The food was good in that none of the items we tasted ended with the words "guts" or "ass," and the town's artisans craft some beautiful Chinese musical instruments. Things were looking up.

Unfortunately, looking up is what usually happens just before you step in a hole. We soon discovered we were on our way to *not* see one of the Chinese New Year celebrations.

Chinese New Year is the largest annual celebration held in this part of the world. Our destination was the town of Ping Shi, where thousands of paper lanterns, heated by candles, would be launched into the night sky. It's reputed to be breathtakingly beautiful, and a big enough deal that the Taiwanese president would be in attendance. The town was in full celebratory mode when we arrived, and even though it was still raining I was certain we would be able to get some good footage.

I should not have been shocked that our van headed in the opposite direction. Rather than dropping us in the middle of the festival we were hauled to the top of a hill and planted at a deserted grammar school. It was here that, hours later, the president was scheduled to speak. We were led into a classroom containing tiny chairs and tiny desks and told that the president would arrive shortly. To pass the time we were given cups of warm soda and sandwiches from a vending machine dating back to the Ming dynasty. Okay, maybe they were made in town earlier that day, but it was hard to tell.

The rain continued to fall, as did darkness. The president had not yet arrived. I informed our guide that Nick and I were leaving. She informed me that the area had been secured for the president's arrival and that all the roads were closed. She took on a look of stern disapproval; I took on a look of "I don't care." Nick and I began hoofing it down the winding road toward the edge of town.

Bus service is free on Chinese New Year, and I recalled seeing loads of people from Taipei being dropped off beyond the barricaded stretch of road. Nick and I managed to hop a bus returning to the city and twenty-five minutes later we were dropped at the Taipei Zoo. We grabbed a taxi, headed to the hotel, and enjoyed a massage, dinner and a good night's sleep.

As things turned out, we would need it.

Explosive Mayhem at the Beehive Festival

The next morning, our guide watching us like a hawk, we packed our gear and boarded Taiwan's high-speed train to the south. We were headed toward the Beehive Festival, a legendary event tied to the Chinese New Year. This is a fireworks display like no other, in that the exploding rockets are fired at participants rather than up into the night sky. It's pyrotechnic masochism taken to an art form. The gist of the event is that a hundred people gather in a circle and allow themselves to be bombarded by hundreds of thousands of bottle rockets. "Use only under adult supervision" has absolutely no meaning at the Beehive Festival, and I was looking forward to getting it all on film.

Or rather, Nick was. I had volunteered to be one of the targets.

Allowing yourself to be assaulted with 100,000 bottle rockets is a little like safe sex. You need protection. As I looked around I noticed that most of the other human targets were locals and predominantly male, men of all ages who had obviously done this before and lived to tell the tale. That observation was not the result of brilliant deductive reasoning on my part; most of the guys wore clothing scarred with burn marks and patches. This was not only a major event for their village; it was a major event for the country. An elevated stage, covered with protective netting, was filled with dozens of cameras that would televise Beehive mayhem all over Taiwan.

Nick headed for the stage and I suited up. I was provided with a fireman's uniform—including jacket, pants and gloves—and a full-coverage motorcycle helmet. This would have been all well and good except for the fact that, at six-foot two inches in height,

Allowing yourself to be assaulted with 100,000 bottle rockets is a little like safe sex.

I'm about eight or ten inches taller than your average Chinese firefighter. I've got long arms, so there was a gap between my gloves and the ends of my sleeves. If I slumped enough to close the gap a space opened up between the bottom of my helmet and the top of the jacket. I resigned myself to the fact that I was going to incur a few burns, but taking a rocket up the sleeve seemed far less damaging that having one explode in my throat. Luckily, one of my fellow nutcases noted my predicament and tossed me a wet towel to wrap around my neck.

I began to consider the possibility that maybe this wasn't the smartest thing I had ever done. On the other hand, we hadn't yet captured any decent footage on this trip. Nick, safe behind his netting, was going to try and keep the camera on me during the entire barrage.

The fusillade began, and I was absolutely fine. Nick, on the other hand, was lying flat on his back and moaning in pain. He'd managed to film for all of three seconds before an errant bottle rocket headed off course, snuck through the stage's protective netting and beaned him dead center between the eyes. He was actually lucky, or as lucky as a guy who has just been shot in the head can hope to be. An inch to the right or left and he'd have lost an eye. The rocket bounced off his head before it exploded, or he might have lost both eyes.

As a couple of bystanders and I helped Nick to a nearby ambulance (yes, it was already there) I tried to provide a few words of comfort. I told him that he really needed only one eye to work a camera, and besides, it might add something to our more exotic trips if my cameraman was sporting a patch.

For some reason he wasn't amused.

I dumped my fireman suit, Nick popped a few Aspirin, and we headed back to the minivan that had brought us to the field of slaughter. The day had been a wash, but at least a solid night's sleep would be possible before we jumped the train back to Taipei in the morning.

More Target Practice and the Big Break

Such was not to be. Our host, insightful as always, had decided we would rather hike around the town and stop at the Taiwan version of a dive restaurant for some noodles. Bone tired, we slurped down our dinner and muttered half-heard curses. A nasty rumor began circulating just as we were about to leave. It seemed that we weren't headed back to the hotel at all. Our guide had set up a few more tortures. I think she was enjoying this.

We were going to another fireworks display. One that had been designed especially for us.

There were no beds in our foreseeable futures, no respite from the Beehive festival and no escaping our sadistic, fireworks-loving captor. We wandered outside the noodle joint and were instructed to climb the stairs of a nearby temple dedicated to Zhu Rong, the Chinese god of fireworks.

I tried to explain that Zhu Rongs do not make a right, that a second gunpowder display was not really necessary. My protestations fell on deaf ears. That lack of hearing might have been partially due to a few thousand explosions, but I don't think so.

We were told that the interior of the temple was the only safe place to stand. We were assured that the rockets wouldn't be pointed in that direction because it was a holy site. There was no way in hell I believed this, and I once more suggested we forego this sequel to bottle rocket madness and head back to the hotel. It was already after 11:00 p.m. and the hotel was an hour away. We had to leave the hotel by 6:00 a.m. in order to make the train to Taipei. I figured I'd be lucky to catch five hours of sleep if we left at that moment, so I pushed for us to get moving. The rest of our group was in full agreement, but there was no way our guide was going to let that happen.

I think I now understand how the Chinese culture has outlasted virtually all others. They just smile a lot and pretend they haven't heard a word you said. Eventually you give up trying and relax to the inevitable.

The fireworks began, and as could have been predicted, most of the rockets headed our way. I guess the god of fireworks was either on vacation or wasn't that highly respected. Temple or not, we were under attack. Rockets whizzed into and through the temple, ricocheting off walls and exploding with a disconcerting echo. I figured that if I didn't lose an eye or a finger I would die of smoke inhalation. More rockets whizzed past our heads, caroming off stairs, pillars and people. I'm pretty sure Nick started having flashbacks.

We couldn't hide from the smoke, but I was doing my best to hide from the rockets. I found a spot toward the back of the temple that seemed to be safe, only to hear our guide call out that I was "missing" the display.

This lasted till well after midnight, By 1:00 a.m., beaten, burned and exhausted, we were in the van and heading toward our hotel. My relief turned to concern when the bus, barely underway, made a turn on a side road to head into another village for a "special" display put on just for us. That was it. Sometimes you can push a prisoner only so far. This was mutiny.

In other words, I lost it. I became Spartacus of the Minivan

"You invited us here so we could report on some great things people might be able to do here, but now you are making it literally impossible for us to do that!" I raised my voice and told the guide. "You are going to take this van, turn it around, and take us back to the %#$@^& hotel now!"

Our driver, tired himself and probably none too keen to be hauling around a group of folks who seemed capable of murderous intent, repeated the same sentiments in Mandarin. Our guide instructed him to drive straight to the hotel. The fear of bad press probably scared her more than anything else.

At that moment I had had enough of this scripted adventure. If I wanted unscripted, then I required a drastic change of plot. The next morning, as Nick and I waited to board the train, I told him we would be peeling off from the group. He agreed, and we checked out some hotel options on our phones as we made our way back toward Taipei.

I thanked our host for her help and apologized for my outburst the night before. The most important thing I did was to make sure she understood we'd be exploring Taipei on our own. She cajoled, protested and promised us the moon, but we weren't buying it. We parted ways roughly five seconds after the train reached the station. I felt like a free man.

It was time to see the sites and hear the sounds of Taipei... *unscripted.*

10

Thailand and the Great Escape

I love Thailand, especially the people. Well, most of the people. From its sacred temples to the smiles of Bangkok's street vendors, the entire nation radiates a mystical quality that I find enchanting. Still, like most places it is not immune to a few profoundly annoying individuals—in this case one particular stone-faced and sadistically focused woman who gave me a case of Southeast Asian Agita nearly the entire time I was there. Is there a vaccination for that? Sadly, no, though I eventually discovered a treatment.

In January of 2010 we traveled to this exotic kingdom to film segments all over the country. We started with a few days in Bangkok then traveled to Chiang Mai, Chiang Rai and Phuket. Instead of the usual guide—someone who would help us create our unscripted moments on the fly with some background or insights, the Government of Thailand provided us with a decidedly different personality for our trip. I can't recall her name, or maybe I'm just suppressing it, but let's just call her *Markie de Sade*. She was probably just doing her job, but in reality she was making ours a lot harder. I'm not saying Markie enjoyed torturing us, but I wouldn't have been surprised if there was a whip inside her Gucci purse.

In some countries, bureaucrats rule, and when it came to the film department of Thailand, bureaucracy appeared to be setting new international standards—doing what bureaucrats do on a Gold Medal level—the kind of place where no document was considered official until it had so many signatures it looked like a get-well card for Dick Cheney.

Hey, as people who travel the world with professional camera and sound gear, we are used to bureaucratic oversight. However, the officialdom got irritatingly personal after we landed at the airport in Bangkok. After more than twenty-four hours of nonstop travel, I desperately needed to shower and change, but Markie had other plans. "No time for shower," she snapped. "Must go to Grand Palace. NOW!" From doing this so many times I can tell you that once you are cleared to film in most places, as we were in Thailand, an hour on either end won't make a difference, but that didn't matter to Madame de Sade.

I tried to explain that I do on-camera work and it wouldn't be good for either me, the destination or anyone with minimal olfactory function if I did my segments while looking (and smelling) like I got hit by a busload of water buffalo. Still, Markie insisted that an appointment had been made and we must honor it.

As we were about to learn, the concept of "appointments" would become a big part of our dozen days here. Ironically, the vast majority of these so-called "appointments" had nothing to do with meeting anyone. They were simply preordained times that we were expected to be at a particular site in order to shoot something, including the Grand Palace, the official residence of Thailand's king. There was no one to interview at these places, and nobody to escort us around to provide commentary. We were simply showing up to shoot video, and time mattered little, at least from our perspective. Markie, who subscribed to the Benito Mussolini School of Time Management, didn't agree.

For her, the world revolved around the *Schedule* and these *Appointments*. In a handful of cases they were necessary, in most they were not. That's why things grew a bit contentious over several days, as Markie's persnickety Schedule became more important than what we actually were there to shoot. It was like having a little mini-director along with us instructing us on what shots to get.

That style doesn't work for us, based on how we produce content and what we believe people are truly interested in when it comes to travel. Indeed, it wouldn't work for anyone, but Markie "Spiel-berg" de Sade didn't have the first clue as to what would work on video.

What she clearly didn't understand is that there are only so many ways to shoot a palace, temple or other historic site. In a country like Thailand, which is full of such places, once you've captured the main sites, *more* palaces and temples didn't equal more experiences. At that point you need to dive deep into the experiences of being in such an exotic locale.

We shoot from the hip, literally. Perhaps that's what frustrated Markie. We didn't intend to follow any script—certainly not hers. But that didn't stop her from barking orders, nipping at our heels. "Take picture of elephant, not little girl," she ordered. "Over here!" she demanded.

So, straight from the airport to the Grand Palace we went. Instead of doing some kind of introduction or on camera commentary, I simply wandered behind my crew as they shot B-roll. As if being tired and smelly weren't enough, we now found ourselves baking in the hot sun with me doing my best to find the shadows. That deferred shower danced tantalizingly in my thoughts as we wandered around the palace grounds, taking in the amazing architecture as well as the jade Buddha that sat in the adjoining temple. A short prayer directed at the Buddha didn't get us back to the hotel any faster, but it did make me feel a little better.

Bug Appetit

My blesséd shower finally came a few hours after our forced march to the Grand Palace. Then we were able to regroup to check out the nightlife in Bangkok, a city of more than nine million residents.

One of the things you'll find on Bangkok's streets are vendors hawking everything you can imagine, from food and household goods to items that are a little more exotic. We started with a visit to Khao San Road. This is a one-kilometer strip of budget hotels, guesthouses, massage parlors, tattoo shops, bars, restaurants and clubs. The popular book *The Beach* described Khao San as "the center of the backpacking universe." It's also featured in the movie by the same name.

Walking along Khao San Road, I ventured into a unique massage experience. No, it's not what you are thinking. This massage was the hands-free variety but did involve feet.

Any ideas?

How about a fish massage? I placed my feet in a plastic kiddie pool filled with hungry little fish. Their meal? The dead skin on my feet. I'd love to say that it was an intensely sensual experience but the truth is that the nibbling made it so that I could barely keep my feet in the water long enough for them to do their work. I'm sure the fish really enjoyed it while it lasted. Consider it to be part of your "exfoliation spa experience" and give it a try on your next visit. That is, if your endurance is better than mine!

With my feet feeling a bit tingly and, um…fishy, it was time for something more adventurous. I headed up the street, and didn't have to go far before running into the Bug Man. No, this guy didn't have tentacles, bulging eyes or a hundred legs, but his cart did. It boasted a bunch of little compartments—a sort of bug tenement, as it were, teaming with such delights as edible wax worms (think oversized maggots), grasshoppers, crickets and even scorpions.

Okay, I admit that this isn't for everyone. It might help to have a couple of beers, if not an entire keg, before chomping down on your first bug. I had eaten bugs, including dragonflies, at the

Fish massage, anyone?

Audubon Insectarium in New Orleans a couple of years earlier. That was a controlled environment where the critters are prepared gourmet style in a kitchen. (Not exactly up to Paul Bocuse's standards, but tasty nonetheless.) This experience was going to be quite a bit different, to say the least.

The bug menu on Khao San Road was a bit more challenging than the *gastro-insectus* experience in N'awlins, because it included a plump scorpion that was almost as long as my hand and fingers. Nick, who didn't chew on anything more exotic than chicken satay, thought it would make a great segment for me to chow down on a couple of bugs and then to swallow the scorpion. Easy for him to say!

Ditching Madame de Sade

After a few nights in Bangkok we set off for Chiang Mai in the north. Instead of a warm and very busy city we'd be venturing to a place that was a bit more relaxed and certainly cooler, espe-

Eating bugs at the Audubon Insectarium in New Orleans.

Perusing the bug menu on Khao San Road.

cially at night. I was excited to experience something new, but even more excited to connect with a different guide for the next leg of our journey.

It was my understanding that we would meet up with someone new in Chiang Mai and leave Madame de Sade and her cat o' nine tails behind. I was imagining an easy-going, flexible and exotically attractive guide who might join me on camera to discuss things related to the experience of the moment. Imagine my dismay when we were picked up for our transfer to the airport and our dominatrix was riding in the front seat of the van!

Oh, well, I thought. She's just accompanying us to the airport. It will all be over shortly. When we arrived, I practically jumped out of the van and felt more energy than I had in days. I gave her and her sidekick a very enthusiastic "Thank you for all of your help ..." grabbed my bags and started toward the airport door. *Free at last!*

I glanced back momentarily and an unpleasant shock lit up my spinal cord, as if those little man-eating carp back on Khao San Road were now nibbling at my nether regions. Pulling up the rear, with a roller bag in tow, was Madame de Sade!

I turned to Nick and said "Looks who's coming."

The color drained from his face. "Oh, no" is all he could muster.

"I think I'm going to kill myself," I said.

Then I had another thought. *Kill Markie!* Well, not exactly *kill* her—although several vivid scenarios along that line had already played in my imagination. Still, I started to get those thoughts that bad people have—you know, like…I could trip her as she steps on the escalator. Just to make it so she needs to take a day or two off work, you understand. I would never wish any serious injury on her or anyone else. A stubbed toe or a lightly twisted ankle might do the trick.

Is that wrong? Yes, it is, and that's why I simply resigned myself to a few more days with this woman. At least the last few days in Phuket would be on our own, or so I thought.

In Chiang Mai, she was all over us. Whether we went out to do a zip-line adventure or simply to peruse the market, we always had company. By the second night we decided to make a run for it. When Markie asked about our filming plans that evening we feigned fatigue and told her that we were just going to relax and stay in. She seemed to buy this excuse because we had been going nonstop for several days at this point.

Thankfully, she was staying at a different property so we simply had to wait until she was driven off to begin our own adventure.

Then, as soon as the coast was clear, we made our move and lit out.

We freely wandered the streets of Chiang Mai, where previously empty sidewalks were now covered with street vendors for their night market. We took some different shots and tried a variety of food until we decided to head back to the hotel. The newfound freedom was glorious, and I felt as if I had finally reached the promised land!

Then it all came crashing down again. On our return to the hotel we were intercepted by Madame de Sade who treated us like teenagers who had broken into the liquor cabinet. I tried the "We found some energy and didn't want to bother you..." routine, but she wasn't buying it. As a result, she tightened the proverbial leash that would keep us within sight until we made it back to Bangkok.

Turning the Tables

De Sade's tightened grip was evident on our drive from Chiang Mai to Chiang Rai. These two destinations are roughly five hours apart, but we were informed that we would be making a side trip to a temple and then *another* palace. It didn't matter that we couldn't film inside any of these places. An Appointment had been made!

The first temple was on our way, so we let Markie win this battle and saved our ammunition for the next one. However, as we learned more about where this second stop was located, I began to push back in earnest. It would be about four hours of additional driving if we were to make this side trip. According to her description, there was nothing incredibly notable about the temple and one thing made the side trip particularly unnecessary: The site was under renovation! I'm not saying if you've seen one Thai temple, you've seen them all, but you get the idea. Markie didn't.

"We're going to head straight to Anantara Resort," I said.

"We have appointment. We must go to the next temple," she replied.

"Sorry, but that's not going to happen."

"We have to go," she snarled, eyes narrowing.

"No…we don't *have* to go anywhere and we certainly aren't going to drive four hours out of the way to a place that most tourists won't be traveling to anyway," I said.

You could almost see the steam coming out of her ears.

"You don't want to show Thai culture?" she demanded.

"Everything we are doing involves Thai culture," I calmly explained. "We have control over what we shoot and how we shoot it. That's how this works."

We were on our way to Anantara and a turning point had been reached. Madame de Sade had finally gotten the message. We didn't need another director. As we arrived a little later at Anantara we quickly scouted the property and decided to shoot an overview. We captured great video from a beautiful resort in the hills of Chiang Rai.

Even though this wasn't planned or even considered ahead of time, it turned out to be a good opportunity that we didn't want to pass up. We need to be flexible and have the ability to change things at the last minute as we see fit. It's another reason we retain creative control and don't simply work as a production company to produce specific content. Because, let me tell you, when you go down that road, everyone you meet on the client side is the next Spielberg. They will start looking at your shots and making suggestions, most of which don't make any sense.

Just ask Nick. I've been guilty of giving him "tips" on what to do next. I'll start in about how which direction we should shoot or how he should come in tighter on something. I'll talk to him about zooming in or out in a particular shot or how to place his camera in just the "right way." In the early days he would politely listen as I wasted valuable time. Every once in a while I'd get something right and he'd let me know. Most of the time, he would wait till I finished talking and then tell me why it wouldn't work. He's just a really polite guy.

Over time, though, Nick and I have formed an "understanding" like an old married couple. When he gives me a sideways look and a shake of his head, I know I've reached the "that's enough" point and he isn't listening anymore. That's why it usually ends up on me to get that message across to anyone who tries to tell him how to do his job. It's a fine balance between making people feel that they are part of the process while not letting them get in the way. Most of the time it works out and every-one comes to a solid understanding.

In Thailand, we never reached that point of understanding with Madame de Sade. Still, we did what we could, and ultimately made sure that we captured as much of the country's essence—*the true experience*—as was humanly possible in the time frame that we traveled.

I just hope and pray that I never again have to step off a plane, boat, bus, sports car or mule—or (heaven forbid) out of my office—and come face to face with the likes of the now-legendary Markie De Sade. I would rather eat a scorpion.

11

Bad Boys in Bangkok

Nick Choo and I most definitely get some looks when we travel together to locales around the globe. Let's face it: I'm a middle-aged guy accompanied by another dude who looks far junior to me and much younger than his actual age. It's often just the two of us, so people we encounter often jump to the conclusion that if we are traveling together, we must *be* together. Let's make it official right now. I'm not gay, not that there is anything wrong with that. Neither is Nick. We are both married and no, we are not operating on the *down low*, as pop culture tends to describe married guys who go out and frequent the gay scene.

But that doesn't stop those looks. Picture this: We are at a resort like Sandals, one that caters specifically to couples and romantic getaways. It's always a beautiful setting, with the tropical breeze moving the branches of nearby palm trees and the Caribbean Sea and sand just steps away. As the sun goes down the atmosphere becomes even lovelier with white-glove dining in an outdoor setting enhanced by candlelight. Nick and I arrive and the hostess has that puzzled look on her face, especially if she didn't see us filming all over the property earlier that day. We take our seats and make small talk as couples all around us are staring into each other's eyes and whispering playfully. Many of these couples have arrived directly from their wedding day, or even got hitched at the resort. Romance is in the air. So what about us?

You can see what I mean.

In some countries and specific locales being gay can be dangerous. These are typically intolerant places where many are afraid to be open about their sexuality for fear of physical harm, or in some cases, death. In those places Nick will actually bring his larger camera and equipment to dinner, providing a sort of prop that indicates "Hey, we are actually here to work and aren't on some kind of date!"

Imagine what it's like to feel open discrimination like that. I get a taste of it when people draw the wrong conclusions about Nick and me. In some cases I see a bemused reaction and in others I see open hostility. That's a disturbing reality that is hard to fathom as an open-minded individual who believes in live and let live. It's akin to standing on a street corner in Manhattan and hailing a cab. If you are black, you'll see empty cabs pass you by as they practice open discrimination. I've witnessed that myself.

Prior to my travels I'd never been the target of discrimination, hostility or plain old mistaken identity. Now I have. Not all of the reactions are hostile, but many are opportunistic and some are even humorous. I learned a lesson about that one night when Nick and I had a chance to explore Bangkok, widely regarded as the sex capital of the world.

The Sex Warehouse

It was the mid-1990s and I was in Bangkok attending the American Society of Travel Agents World Travel Congress. Each day started at the convention center where travel agents would interact with suppliers and destinations that were exhibiting at a trade show. We also had a booth so we could connect with our readers as well as the advertisers who supported our publications.

Right next to our booth was one occupied by a major car rental company, and every day in that booth was a guy named Jim, who we spoke to frequently over the course of the week. On the first day Jim looked like a professional on top of his game. His eyes were clear and he had a great deal of energy. As the week progressed, however, Jim started to change. His eyes became more bloodshot, the circles under them becoming larger and darker.

Each day he would tell me about the previous night's adventures on the teeming streets of the city. One place that stood out in particular was Pad Pong, Bangkok's renowned marketplace and strip club neighborhood. Most mornings at the show, a bedraggled but strangely satisfied Jim would regale me with stories from Pad Pong that went beyond interesting, and in some cases were rather disgusting. For instance, I learned during the week of the various ways you can play ping pong, or a version of it, with the female employees at one of these bars. I also learned about a hands-free ways for them to drink a Coke where the bottle never got near the girl's mouth, but the beverage still ended up inside of her.

I also learned about a new way to play darts and how Jim almost lost an eye. Imagine being able to "throw" one of these little missiles without ever touching it with your hands. Okay, maybe you don't really want to think about that, or the fact that Jim almost lost an eye when one of those things zoomed past his head. Or maybe you just want to consider the fact that he jumped, not from the dart itself, but the sound of the balloon bursting behind his head when the dart struck it.

Was my curiosity piqued? You bet it was. I couldn't believe the stories I was hearing and knew that I had to see this debauchery firsthand. Unfortunately, my days were filled with the trade show while my evenings were booked with client dinners. By the time those dinners ended I was on my way to bed because I had another long day to face in the morning. Under those circumstances, I wasn't going to witness any deviant behavior first-hand, though I certainly felt that I was living vicariously through Jim's daily updates.

But as the week wore on my resistance lowered. The world's a big place, I figured, and when would I be back in Bangkok in the future? It so happened that on my final day there I had an afternoon and evening completely free ahead of my overnight flight to the United States. So, I hired a driver and car at the hotel and set out with my then-marketing director to see this seedier side of the city.

Our plan was to first check out a couple of the mainstream tourist highlights, like the Grand Palace, and then do some shopping before heading to Pad Pong. Prior to departing from the hotel the doorman gave instructions to our female driver as to where to take us. She got the first two stops right, hitting the palace and a shopping area, but went off the rails on the third.

We weren't sure where she had taken us when we pulled up into an empty parking lot in front of a large gray building. Picture a soviet era building, with no details and a drab gray exterior. I don't recall seeing windows, only two doors at the top of a set of steps. It certainly wasn't what I was expecting. There was no way this was the fabled Pad Pong, I thought.

I tried to have a conversation with the driver, but to no avail. She used her hand to point toward the entrance of the building while we shifted in our seats and tried to figure out our next move. She didn't seem to understand that we were in the wrong spot, but was politely quiet as the two of us looked at each other, shrugged and jumped out of the car. I gave our driver the "be right back" universal sign and headed toward the steps.

The descriptions of bar girls and neon signs seemed a universe away from the drab monolith that rose in front of us. With our driver not speaking any English, and us not understanding a word of Thai, the next best step seemed to be querying somebody in this official-looking building. In the worst case they could let our driver know where we really wanted to go, I figured.

We half expected to see some kind of business-style reception area when we entered the building, but that expectation couldn't have been more off. As we walked in we immediately noticed a glassed-in room to our left, filled with what had to be fifty women. They were all wearing pastel-colored dresses and each had a round button with a large number on it. It took about a millisecond to understand that we had been brought to a large-scale whorehouse and not some bar on the streets of Bangkok. Office building? The only work being completed here had nothing to do with papers and white collars.

We immediately started to back out, and were intercepted by a short, older woman who practically flew out from behind a small desk area.

"Why are you leaving?" she demanded. "You just get here."

"We're in the wrong place. We thought we were coming to a place where the girls dance and do other things," I replied.

"They will do whatever you want," she explained.

"That's okay, but this isn't what we want," I told her.

"What do you want, a massage? Two girls?"

We couldn't get out of there fast enough. It was like we were suddenly inserted into a segment that *60 Minutes* had done around the same time on the sex trade in Asia. Indeed, it seemed like one of the scenes from that segment could have been this exact place. It was both disturbing and sad at the same time as many of these women were probably teenagers who didn't have much of a choice in the lives they were currently leading.

A Case of Mistaken Identity

I never forgot that experience and certainly didn't want to repeat it. I never did make it to Pad Pong on that trip, but roughly fifteen years after that final night in Bangkok I found myself back in the same city. This time I was here for a different reason that had nothing to do with trade shows or the infamous sex trade.

I had come to explore four areas in the country, including Chiang Mai, Chiang Rai, Phuket and of course, Bangkok. Our journey began there with three nights in a five-star hotel. On our first night we realized that the hotel was a short walk away from Pad Pong. I immediately had a flashback to Jim's bleary-eyed yet smiling face as he explained the many things he had witnessed there all those years ago. I also thought about the drive that my marketing guy and I went on when the driver delivered us to that gray, drab building that turned out to be a whorehouse.

We decided to grab the opportunity and finally explore those infamous streets of Pad Pong. The glittering lights, young women lined up outside the bars, demented games of darts and other diversions beckoned.

We had inquired about the area from the front desk, but the clerk there was not eager to share information about it other than essentially advising us to stay away. It seems that many in the Thai tourism and hospitality world had become sensitive to Bangkok's sex trade reputation and were looking to suppress our curiosity.

In his warnings the clerk explained that these girls would bother us on the street and try to get us into their respective establishments. They would be competing for us to come in and see the sordid show, pay for drinks, provide tips, and God only knows what else. If you ever saw *The Crying Game* or *The Hangover Part II* you might have a clear picture of the "whatever else" that might be possible.

To be frank, the clerk had succeeded in making me a bit nervous, even though his dire scenarios weren't in tune with the many stories I had heard from Jim so many years before. I started to think that maybe the fact that Jim and his colleagues went as a group may have meant strength in numbers and hence no issues regarding safety.

Well, we summoned our manly courage and headed to Pad Pong anyway. When we arrived in the area, the girls who were standing or sitting near the doors of the various clubs paid literally no attention to us. Based on the description we were given, we couldn't believe that they wouldn't be out there swarming us on such a quiet evening, but they weren't. It just didn't happen.

What *did* happen was something that surprised me, but I guess it shouldn't have. As we approached one end of the street a young man swooped in on us, offering something that appeared to be either a CD or a DVD. We didn't speak the language, but his approach didn't seem all that unusual. After all, tourists like us will typically spend money buying souvenirs and other gifts when we travel; it's what makes many of the economies in the world run.

They say that selling comes down to qualifying customers or prospects to see if they are the right targets for the particular offering. This guy had done his homework on the fly and clearly had concluded that we were his target demographic.

As it turns out the item he shoved in front of us wasn't a music CD or even a pirated Hollywood movie. Instead it was a DVD featuring gay porn. No wonder the women weren't paying any attention to us as we walked the street! Apparently everyone there thought we were gay!

We laughed our asses off as the perplexed vendor walked away without making a sale. Somewhat intimidated, we circled the block and then decided to head back to the hotel, wondering when we'd next be in a position to check out what really goes on in these bars.

Our original intent was to sample this experience, perhaps a bizarre strip show or a game of perverted ping pong, but we ended the evening without entering even a single establishment. I was back in my room at an hour that wouldn't have troubled my grandmother, let alone my wife. To add insult to injury, and maybe I was just imagining this, that overly cautious desk clerk seemed to nod approvingly as we walked back through the front doors so soon after we had left. Damn!

The Two-Edged Sword

Why do people make the assumption that two guys walking down the street might be a good target market for gay porn? I think it has to do with the older man with the younger guy situation, although I don't consider myself to be all that old. It's just that Nick looks so young!

How young does Nick look? So young that on numerous occasions I've gotten away with the explanation that we aren't colleagues, but instead father and son. There have been many instances where I've simply introduced Nick to the hostess, waitress or anyone else who will listen as my adopted son from China. I continue on with a story about traveling to an orphanage and finding him when he was just two, and bringing him back to live with my family and me.

Admittedly, most of the time the person we're addressing will just give me that look that says, "C'mon, you're putting me on…" but sometimes I get a very sincere "Wow, that's really neat…!"

Using an ambiguous relationship to mess with people's heads is just one of the ways I entertain myself when I'm on one of my trips. What I learned in Bangkok is that sometimes that same ambiguity can douse the hope of having much fun at all.

I hate to say it, but I think that good old Jim might have been a little disappointed with our performance in Pad Pong, but at least we made that desk clerk happy.

12

Today Show Unscripted

Ted Danson has some *cajones*, I don't mind telling you. Especially when it comes to food, as he shockingly demonstrated in an unscripted moment I witnessed off-camera at the *Today Show*.

We were setting up to shoot a segment with Hoda Kotb and guest host Andy Cohen in one of my many appearances as a travel expert on the iconic morning show. This particular four-minute bit featured food that was quite different from what most westerners would dare eat.

One of the unusual delicacies on the table in front of us was durian, known as the King of Fruit and generally popular in Southeast Asia. Durian might also be referred to as the King of Stink. That's because the smell can be quite overpowering, with descriptions ranging from a city landfill in summer to the smell of rotting meat and dirty socks. That powerful aroma is only part of the fun, as its texture, resembling that of rotting flesh and custard, takes everything else to a new level. A rather unique combination, wouldn't you say?

The shock factor didn't stop there. We had also brought in several other dishes that day, including pig's blood and pig intestine soup. Just the thought of eating the congealed blood of a pig will cause most people to gag. Add in some intestines and you have a real winning combination. Even though this culinary combo may seem odd by American standards, it's actually enjoyed quite widely around the world with some variation—kind of like Baskin-Robbins' 31 Flavors, I suppose.

There were a few other dishes laid out for tasting as well, including something known as Stinky Tofu. If the Durian wasn't smelly enough, the tofu certainly was. This gourmet treat is prepared by basically dumping a bunch of tofu in a bucket of brine that also includes fermented milk and meat, plus some dried shrimp. Once the entire mess has sat for several months the smell is so overpowering you wouldn't even consider bringing it into your home. Then, and only then, are you ready to eat it! Fans of this dish say that the more it smells the better it tastes.

The Today Show's Hoda and Bravo's Andy Cohen try some disgusting delights. (Courtesy of NBC.© 2010. All rights reserved.)

Worms and Salsa

Part of our setup for this show consisted of some worms (yes, *worms*) and salsa along with chips prepared at Bug Appetit in the Audubon Insectarium of New Orleans. We had a bowl each of wax worms and meal worms. Both look less than appetizing, but at least they are prepared in a way that can mask any tastes a person could find offensive. This makes swallowing the crispy critters more of a mind-over-matter situation than a taste issue.

In a move to add to the interactive nature of the segment and to provide a little gross-out factor, we attempted to get some live worms sent along with those that were expertly prepared, but the Insectarium wasn't able to do that. We were stuck with the cooked variety, all in the salsa, until my publicist made a couple of calls.

Those calls resulted in a messenger bringing us live worms from a local pet supply discount store. Now you may be asking yourself, "Why do people buy meal worms?" According to the person at the store, most customers buy them to feed their pet lizards.

Ted's Brunch

As the clock ticked down to the start of the segment I was excited to see how the hosts would handle these special treats. As I waited to go live Ted Danson appeared on the other side of the counter after just finishing up an interview of his own. He was curious to see what we were up to and took a keen interest in the worms that were squirming around.

Ted commented that he wouldn't have a problem eating any of the stuff in front of him, including the live worms, and then proceeded to do just that! As he tossed a live meal worm into his mouth the people on the set at the show gasped, laughed and clapped at his antics. A neutral face on his part quickly gave way to a statement about a "funky aftertaste" as he reached for a glass of water.

As he walked off the set I thought...*whoa, did he just do that?!* And then a second thought occurred to me: He must have thought these were some kind of gourmet-style worms, the kind that are kept in pristine conditions and used in exotic food preparation, similar to what the Insectarium prepares. Sorry Ted, but you moved so fast we didn't even get a chance to wave you off. *Dude, you just ate some lizard's breakfast!*

I got a good chuckle out of Ted's antics and decided to take a look on the Internet following this little interaction. I was curious what they would say about mealworms. I had no idea what to expect because I had only eaten them in the past. Unlike Ted, my experiences occurred with the deceased and "prepared" variety, and took place in locations ranging from the New Orleans Insectarium to the streets of Bangkok. I subsequently did a little research and learned that mealworms are the larval stage of the Darkling Beetle and also are breedable. Gee, maybe I could have been proactive and provided this essential info as a guide to Ted's Adventure that day on *Today*.

Enough said about meal worms! Anyone hungry?

13

The Curse of Kang

When you have the last name of Murphy you grow up very aware of the law named after you. Indeed, Murphy's Law has a number of iterations with my favorite being this: The light at the end of the tunnel is the headlamp of an oncoming train. How great is that? Just as you expect good things to happen, you have another setback. You go from being suddenly energized to back down into the dumps.

To be even more specific, you might, as I have, acquired a certain fear of a rendezvous with the Forces of Darkness. That is, powers that can toss you against your best efforts into the pits of disorder, despair, chagrin, and even complete chaos against your will. What makes this sense of foreboding even more frightening is that it can take place at the hands of a sunny, smiling innocent-looking person who you would least suspect of any connection with the murkier twists in life. In my case, the agency of my visit to Hell took the form of the blank expression of my intrepid video crew member, Gene Kang.

No, he's not a Sherpa, but he plays one on TV.

My tale of the Curse of Kang was actually predicted by a Korean fortune teller. I'm sure it's easy for you to conjure up images of people in my line of work visiting occult locations in the far corners of Asia. The usual stock Hollywood images—Marlene Dietrich held hostage in an Asian opium den, the bizarre mystics in China and the Orient holding forth on buccaneering sea captains with dark forecasts and hints of evil to come. In places like Vietnam or Korea people consult with these individuals to see what lies ahead for themselves and their families. There's a whole aura to the images of fortune telling that one of life's big banana peels is about to turn up and you are going to end up slam bang on your gluts if you don't watch out.

I even went so far as to have my fortune read by a Vietnamese gentleman in northern California. He didn't speak a word of English and I'm not versed in Vietnamese so I sat back as he began to make an assessment. He used my date and time of birth to analyze me and came up with an accurate assessment of who I am and what I'm about. It was surprisingly accurate, to say the least. I went in with skepticism and came out a believer to some extent. It was a very strange experience.

Keep this firmly in mind now that I turn to the sinister peregrinations of this Kang.

Let me say, at the outset, that Gene Kang is a nice guy. If you just looked at him though, you might think he's a little bit sinister. The detailed tattoo running down his left arm and his pumped-up bicep makes him seem a little bit intimidating, but that goes away when he opens his mouth. He's a genuinely nice guy who, although very quiet, will open up with a bit of prodding. You might even call him shy.

He's a stealth fashion guy who seems to be always dressed to impress. His hairstyle and clothes stay updated, with his hair changing on a weekly basis. He combines a tough-guy exterior with a fashion sense.

You might even mistake him as a yakuza member, a Japanese gang that's similar to the mafia in our country…even though he's Korean. I could personally see him, as some of the women we come across in Asia do, as a Korean soap opera actor.

On the surface he's a bright stylish piece of work, but deep down beneath that benign, ambient smile, lurks a strange intimate connection with the Twilight Zone.

Around Kang, things have a way of mysteriously going wrong. One minute objects are there, the next minute they are gone, never to be seen again. He is a mystic magician of the *here it is now* and *where the hell did it go?*

Chaos in Israel

The signature incident for this Curse of Kang happened on a trip to Israel when we lost a directional microphone that we use in our filming. Gene was our sound guy on the trip and couldn't locate the microphone after we landed in Tel Aviv. He and producer Nick Choo couldn't understand what happened to it as they were certain it had been packed. We had the tube that held the microphone as well as the sheepskin cover. The only thing missing was the mike itself.

The bottom line was that without this microphone we would have a serious problem in capturing the real-world local interactions that were the very heart of our reporting—like buying something in a market or breaking bread with a local. After all, capturing those person-to-person dialogs were a big reason we were there.

Alarm bells began to go off in my mind that we were lurching rapidly into Chaos Territory. After rummaging through the various bags and items, Kang and Choo came to the conclusion that the airline must have confiscated the item!

If you've ever flown to Israel you'll know what I mean—the security for El Al Airlines is the tightest security you have ever seen. El Al is the country's flag carrier and every step of the way to boarding is complete with profiling you, screening you, searching you and more. If you make it through that you know that *nobody* is getting on that plane with anything that could even resemble a weapon, let alone be one. I never felt safer flying than on that flight from Newark to Tel Aviv.

That's why I looked on in amusement when the confiscation analysis took place. The conversation went like this:

Nick: "Are you *sure* you packed it, Gene?"

Gene: "Definitely. I put it in the case along with the sheath and the holder. It should be there."

Mark: "Well it's definitely not *there* so where do you think it is?"

Gene: "They must have confiscated it at security. I'll bet they thought it was a weapon!"

Mark: "A weapon? You think they are that stupid?"

If you know anything about the crack Israeli security for El Al Airlines, you know that they would not confuse a pole mike with some form of military ordnance.

My chaos theorem now escalated to a larger suspicion that deep within Kang's genetic makeup was a considerable presence of the Oops chromosome. I gently suggested they call the office and sure enough, when Nick got off the phone he said "Gene, it's back at the office sitting on your desk!"

Kang's face went white and he made a noise like a motorcycle backfiring. "Damn" he sighed, throwing his hands in the air. "How the HELL did it manage to get there?"

Hmmm. It suddenly occurred to me that this little incident wasn't just garden-variety forgetfulness. I had a premonition that it had to come from a higher power. It had to be something bigger, greater, even darker. After all, not only did Kang not know where the missing mike was, he seemed to think that it had a mind of its own and it was actually avoiding him.

It was at that moment that the Curse of Kang was born—at some deep level I knew that this well-intentioned young man had been born under some Asian equivalent of a gibbering occult gonzo star. As it turned out, presaged by an as-yet-unknown Korean Fortune teller—I was right!

We as a team had now officially arrived in what I politely refer to as Deep Shit. Here we were in Israel, expecting to be out shooting footage of the experiences, the people and the culture up close and we were lacking one of the key pieces of our equipment to do just that.

I did the rapid "FedEx it here in four days or buy it at budget-buster prices" calculation and opted for the latter. We were stuck for the extra bucks, but it was all chalked up to lessons learned.

Kang's Occult History

It turned out I was channeling a distant Korean Fortune Teller. Unknown to Kang, his mother, who is Korean, traveled back to her home country to spend time with her family. While there she consulted with a fortune teller who shared insights on her as well as her family. She was told that her son "needs to be careful when he travels" as something bad could happen. The mystic told her that Gene needs to be especially careful in the month of March, as this is the height of potential travel issues that can impact him.

There it was. The Curse of Kang was part of Gene's bio-spiritual make up. No matter what he did, no matter how he did it, objects were just fated to misbehave and get lost around him!

For the first time in my career, I was confronted with what I will have to call an occult crisis. Here, on the one hand, I had a genuinely talented production team member—great with a camera, great with setting up a shoot, and excellent at setting up and getting great interview footage in faraway and challenging venues. That's all to the good side.

On the other side, this man Kang was clearly a disaster waiting to happen. In a short time I felt an overpowering instinct to wrap one big "Danger" flag around him every time we got in the airport shuttle to go near an airport with trunks and gear in tow, dreading the next episode of cables and camera gear lost to some virtual Bermuda Triangle that was part of his curse.

For example, on a subsequent trip to Germany his luggage for the return to Philadelphia got lost for several days. When it finally did appear his relatively new suitcase came back looking like it had been chewed over as hot lunch for the Minotaur. Honestly, it was bruised, ripped, disfigured, and damaged beyond recognition. A casual explanation might have been that the thing might have gotten caught in one of those enormous Anaconda-resembling conveyor devices that are so in-fashion with the airlines these days—that would have been easy. But with Kang, I knew it had to be something more. His bag was fated to get trashed. It was written in the stars. You would have thought he had used it for years, but it was only the first trip for this particular bag. When you're cursed, you're cursed.

In some situations, just the proximity of Kang was the trigger for equipment catastrophe. On one shoot an unfortunate Steadicam became the victim of Gene's curse's relationship with the beyond. For those of you who aren't familiar, a Steadicam is a stabilizing device worn by a camera operator that holds the camera and absorbs movement so the image is clean and fluid as the operator walks and moves. It permits very unique and specialized filming and is a highly technical piece of gear that we must fly in with us. You can't pick up a Steadicam at any corner camera store, particularly when you're out in some faraway exotic locale.

We were traveling as a team to the Andalucia region of Spain in March of 2011. Based on past experience I had made sure that none of the Steadicam equipment was in Kang's baggage! The team had packed up all the gear necessary and when we arrived, sure enough, Kang's suitcase never made it to Malaga. But other bags assigned to the rest of the team didn't arrive either. It turned out that Kang had packed these bags! This included a tripod. On top of this, the Steadicam bag, assigned to Nick, had been partially opened and the weights necessary to use this item were nowhere to be found! So we had the entire Steadicam set up and couldn't use it because we were missing the weights that went with it! The weights would fit in your pants pocket, but that didn't much matter as they were simply gone.

We ended up buying a replacement tripod, but had no such luck with the Steadicam. It became an extra few pieces that needed to be hauled around from hotel to hotel as we traveled all over this region of Spain. Each time it was moved from the car to the hotel, and back again, it was a stark reminder of the Curse of Kang.

At one point Kang casually mentioned how his mother's fortune teller had predicted difficulties in his travels. The timing, March, and the revelation of the related predictions, led us to what was, and still is, the Curse of Kang.

The Curse of Kang—Hyperdrive

I have to admit that none of the things that actually happened to Gene Kang and the production team were in themselves really that bad. They cost the team a few extra bucks, we lost time and, in some cases, we lost some key shots, due to the lack of vital equipment on location.

But what the Curse of Kang did was to install a panic button in my soul. It was not about what *did* actually happen…it was all about what *could* happen—and who knows what dire circumstances could flow from Kang's eerie communion with the slapstick nature of the Forces of Darkness? I found myself obsessed with dark meditations on what might take place if Kang's Ooops chromosome got triggered by the Dark Side with a few random trolls from the unknown thrown in for good measure to create something really exquisitely awful. Well, see for yourself.

The Curse of Kang in Hyperdrive

Potential Alarming Situation	Curse Engaged	Immediate Disaster	Catastrophic Outcome
Team shooting ancient ruins in transitional junta-ruled communist regime.	Kang in custody of bag containing team passports.	Confuses passport bag with lunch recycling bag full of leftover Lo Mein Bok Choy and bottled water.	Glowering local constabulary demands interview with production team; consulate summoned.
Team holds production meeting discussing annoyance with their state-appointed chaperone.	Kang accidentally leaves iPhone channel open to chaperone during entire meeting.	Chaperone arrives with armed military detachment.	Production team settles for hostage exchange at the border.
Team requests shooting rights in small proud South American town.	Kang composes request which when translated includes the phrase "this town barks like an unfortunate yellow canine."	Team hastily examines exit strategies and assesses Jeep acceleration speeds.	Kindly local mounts imbecility defense for team and barely averts bloodshed.
Team shoots amusing Sangria-fueled outtakes telling everybody's favorite party jokes and adventures with former girlfriends.	Kang posts all of the videos on the production team update site.	Unwanted fame arrives in the form of shrieking emails the next morning	Divorce counselors engaged.
Team shoots rare primitive Asian temple cult rituals never before recorded.	Kang puts on sacred antlers and begins to follow along with temple dances performed by attractive cultists.	Priests inform Kang he could serve as a propitious human sacrifice candidate for fertility goddess.	Kang does Olympic ditch dash into nearest jungle hideout.
Team is shooting a gathering of delegates to an international peace conference.	Kang is assigned to mike each of the principal delegate seats and staff the sound board.	Kang's failure to mute mike at coffee break leads to full open-mike assessment of delegate opinions of each other on PA system.	CNN Breaking News: Wolf Blitzer opines that the conference has set back world peace by ten years.

14

Are You Smarter than a Fifth Grader?

When we approach a segment, we first sit back and listen to the perspective of those who know far more than we do about any particular attraction or destination. Many times that person is the guide who is traveling with us or meeting us on location. Sometimes it is the general manager or director of the actual attraction. On some occasions we rely on a local we happen to run into in a particular restaurant or bar.

I seek out that insider's knowledge no matter where I am. To put it bluntly, I'm an information whore. I'll go to anyone, anytime and in any place to learn what I can about what we are trying to showcase. I might ask for some background, question those answers to get even more information, and then use what I learn to describe with detail what we are shooting at any given moment.

We lean on any and all resources because, as they say, necessity is the mother of invention. The necessity for us is the brutal fact that we don't have an advance team that maps out our shots, or even our topics, prior to jumping on a plane and jetting off to sites not yet seen. Invention is what we do. We invent a script on the fly and do our best to give you a great perspective on our experience.

I had to rely on a little invention when I wanted to do a segment on Yellowstone during our Grand Luxe rail trip. This journey put you on a luxury train that takes you to different national parks beginning in New Mexico and ending in Wyoming.

We were nearing the end of our trip with a stop in Yellowstone National Park and were trying to decide what to shoot as our final segment there. We had already been to what's known as the Thermal (Fountain) Paint Pots, an area where you can see the four different thermal features that make up Yellowstone, all in one location. As you walk along a small boardwalk that gets you up close to these geologic wonders, you see geysers, hot springs, mud pots and fumaroles.

They call these paint pots because they have a variety of different colors that are created by bacteria. The older the particular thermal feature is, the more colorful it becomes, or so they told me. What they didn't have to tell me was the fact that it smells like rotten eggs. Simply get a nice downwind breeze and your gag reflex might kick in. My high school science classes paid off here, as I was able to comment on the origin of this smell without having to tap the insight of the local guide or anyone else. I was in my element because I managed to stay awake in chemistry class and could even recall the name of the chemical compound that threw off that nasty smell: hydrogen sulfide.

How does one stay awake in chemistry class? Just make sure the topic is related to potty humor and you'll capture most of the kids' attention, especially the boys. Maybe it's the fact that I was once a boy and all boys think that things that smell bad are really funny.

Indeed, tell me one boy out there, and most adult men, who don't delve into the improper etiquette of toilet humor. The case of rotten eggs fits nicely into this fact of male nature, yet I managed to keep it clean for the video.

Kid Commentator

Like many tours, and this *was* a tour in the traditional sense, we hopped back on our motor coach and left this area to experience a few others. One stop brought us down another boardwalk to a large lake that had water boiling in different areas. The temperature of this lake is said to average 158 degrees Fahrenheit. That's something to consider when most hot tubs are quite warm when set to 103 degrees Fahrenheit and take a little easing into to adapt to the temperature.

The day's final stop brought us to the main lodge right next to a site that most people are familiar with, Old Faithful. This geyser gets its name from the fact that it reliably goes off every sixty to ninety minutes to give observers a glimpse into the geological wonder that lies below. As we stood there waiting for the geyser to build up for its next blastoff, Nick and I discussed what we might do to provide a perspective. We were basically on our own and struggling with what we might say.

The challenge comes down to what you can say about a geyser that everyone hasn't already learned about or seen on television. Quite simply, there isn't much to say. The picture, or in this case the video, does most of the talking.

Instead of focusing on the geyser, it made more sense to provide a little bit of the history of Yellowstone and what actually created these geological wonders that we were experiencing on the surface. Only catch? I really didn't know enough to add to the conversation right at that moment. My knowledge didn't go far

My fifth grader proved to be a Yellowstone Park expert.

beyond the basics that I had already shared, so what could I introduce that might be different and still be insightful? I was stuck.

Then I had one of those "aha" moments. I saw my son standing off to the side and realized he might be the key to my conundrum. This kid had just finished fifth grade, and you know what that means!

If you ever saw the TV show *Are You Smarter than a Fifth Grader,* you'll know why I quickly yelled "Hey Jack, come over here for a minute." I asked him if he'd like to share some knowledge on Yellowstone, and he was willing to work for me, royalty free!

I started with a basic question about Yellowstone and his answer surprised me. He was very much aware of what led to the formation of this area and what might happen in the future.

Instead of simply pumping the kid for information and then turning around and using it to make myself appear smart, I went ahead and put him on camera. Here's what we discussed in our brief interview:

Mark: So while I'm here in Yellowstone, I want to ask you, are you smarter than a fifth grader? I know I'm not, and this is a fifth grader here named Jack. Jack, tell us why or what causes all this steam you see here in Yellowstone, in particular those geysers that go off here regularly.

Jack: Well Yellowstone Park is actually a huge super-volcano, which is basically a big buildup of magma underneath the surface.

Mark: And that's what's causing the heat that causes the steam and these hot springs? That's interesting. Now how long ago did this super-volcano erupt and literally form Yellowstone?

Jack: Around 650,000 years ago.

Mark: Okay so around 650,000 ago, which means...are we coming up on another eruption anytime soon?

Jack: Yeah, in another 100,000 years.

Mark: Okay. I guess we've got a little time to wait on that one and I'm glad we're not going to be around in another 100,000 years, but if we were, what are the chances that this volcano would wipe out a good portion of the United States?

Jack: Well, the western half of the country will be covered in three feet of ash and it will send the world into an ice age for thousands of years.

Mark: Well okay. We're glad that we're not going to be here in another hundred thousand years I guess.

There you have it! I certainly didn't have those answers readily available and didn't have any other source for it as I stood and surveyed the area. My fifth grader was able to step in and close out our segment with some fun commentary that made this dad proud.

15

Bureaucracy Is Everywhere

Creating an episode of *Travel Unscripted* is usually fun and relatively straightforward. We show up and we shoot. We focus on the people and our experiences, things that can't be captured when they're rehearsed or canned. We thrive on discovering the offbeat and unusual. It works great, for us, to film spontaneously, discovering the highs and lows of a destination.

Unfortunately that's not such a popular philosophy among many of the various and sundry career bureaucrats who control entry into some of the countries we wish to visit. Some of these folks have never seen a Potemkin village they didn't love, and seem absolutely terrified that we might record an event that portrays their home as anything less than the Garden of Eden. It's okay, in their mind, to take staged pictures of smiling monks tending to grape vines. It's a nightmare of infinite proportions, however, to catch one of those same monks stealing a smoke or taking a piss in the shadow of a Buddha statue.

Such being the case, my motto has become, "Don't ask for permission, ask for forgiveness."

There's a reason for this. Pleading ignorance after the fact generally results in nothing more than wagging fingers, dirty looks and admonitions about "how things are normally done." We act contrite, promise to follow the rules, wander off, and do whatever we damned well please. Asking for permission before the fact, stating that your intention is to meander about and film anything you find interesting, is the ultimate nonstarter.

Here's a fact of life: Give a career civil servant even the slightest opportunity to say "no" and you can bet your bottom dollar he or she will oblige. Even the most lowly assistant to the Superintendent of Toilet Paper Replenishment at a nation's Ministry of Extramarital Affairs can derail your best-laid plans. He can deny your visa, bury you in paperwork, or worst of all…ask for a script and an itinerary.

That's a problem. We don't do scripts and itineraries.

Our typical *modus operandi* is to do an end-run around the bureaucrats by providing them with something that broadly states our objectives without providing any sort of concrete detail. Having a paper trail of this nature satisfies most government lackeys; it gives them plausible deniability should we air something that irritates their boss or supervisor.

How to BS a Bureaucrat

My producer generally sends the bureaucrat in question a letter such as the following. (I'm providing our official line of bull, along with our private definition of the official line of bull.)

- The focus of the videos will be a showcase of your lovely and exciting country. We will provide a contemporary look at the professional and expert manner in which "The Tour Operator" provides travel experiences to the destination. Mark Murphy will experience the tours firsthand, and the videos will be a document of his experiences. The tour will visit "these major areas."

(If you leave us alone we will provide a very nice "Thank You" in the credits. We have no plans to collect footage of your country's prime minister leaving a strip club specializing in she-males and attractive sheep. On the other hand, we'll probably interview a food kiosk proprietor known for his unique Hamster-on-a Stick recipe.)

- During the trip Mark will inform U.S. travel agents and consumers about transportation, travel conditions, and interesting and unusual sights. We will highlight some of the great hotel properties available to visitors under "The Tour Operator's" program. The videos will immerse the viewer in the experience provided at "The Destination."

(By allowing us to do our thing you'll end up with a unique series of Travel Unscripted *episodes that will highlight the experiences in your country. Failure to do so may mean a possible exposé of your underground slave trade.)*

- The videos will focus on the traditional sites and interesting cultural activities.

(Because you control our visas we will make three-minute stops at most of the historical monuments you suggest. We will then check them off the list and get down to the real reason we are here.)

- Mark will go to these sites and talk about the history, showcase the attractions, interact with the locals, sample the local cuisine and immerse himself in the destination to enhance the viewer's experience and pique his curiosity.

(We will stop at the aforementioned monuments, meet the nonlocals you have trucked in, eat the provided food that is not normally there, and refrain from in-depth interviews with lepers who have a desire to change their spots. Then, we'll leave as quickly as possible and film the parts of your country that are actually interesting.)

- The title of our show and concept is *Travel Unscripted*, essentially a reality documentation of Mark Murphy's travels through your country. This aligns with the current trend of marketing in the United States.

(Don't try and interfere with our filming, editing or marketing. We do this for a living and the last time we checked you weren't showing up in the credits for a Steven Spielberg movie. It's really great that you discovered the wheel. Now, go away.)

- The goal is to bring "The Destination" to life for travel agents and consumers in the United States. Our primary objective is to provide insight into something more than the "The Destination" as depicted on the typical travel brochure. Via interaction with the local people, and by documenting interesting experiences, we will show potential visitors the warm, friendly and mysterious charms of your country.

(We brought our own penicillin. But thanks for the offer.)

Dealing with the Chairman

Overtures such as this usually gain us entry into the countries we seek to explore…but not always. The worst kind of bureaucrat is one who takes his job seriously, and that's exactly who we were dealing with as we planned a trip to yet another nation that shall remain unnamed in these pages. This guy—let's just call him

"Chairman Forked-Tung"—was an utterly unreasonable bastard who was obviously bucking for promotion to Chief Deputy in Charge of Pencil Shavings. The Chairman wanted a detailed plan outlining every place we planned to stop and everything we planned to shoot. He acted like it was 1975 and we were CIA insurgents. For six months his requests and our answers had been flying back and forth.

We were already three months behind schedule, and for all practical purposes we remained at square one. Paranoia is a terrible thing when it resides in the mind of a government bootlicker, and The Chairman apparently saw potential disaster in even the most simple of requests. We were about to throw in the towel when my producer decided to make a final attempt at negotiations.

Though it went against both his and my grain, we decided to try and come up with an itinerary. We listed the cities and regions where we planned to stop. We suggested an outline of events and sights we hoped to shoot. Granted, we didn't set any of this in stone—mostly because we just wanted to get into the country and then start filming whatever struck our fancy—but we strongly implied that our handler would know our basic actions and whereabouts.

The Chairman was having none of it. He sent me a fax that read, in part, as follows.

Dear Mr. Murphy:

The Division of Semi-Sanitary Napkins, which operates under the auspices of the Ministry of Sidewalk Quality Assurance, which is headed by General Musharaff and his pet rabbit, requires a more detailed script that includes your truthful purpose, an itinerary broken down by day and time, any spe-

cific highlights you might wish to showcase, the length of the final film, and the outlets on which it will be aired. The General's rabbit further requires detailed CVs of the filming team, including but not restricted to their past experiences, blood types, hobbies, noticeable scars or tattoos, sexually transmitted diseases, weight, height, hair color and naked pictures of their last three ex-wives with plastic buckets over their heads.

The Chairman went on to say that he needed a list of all equipment we might be bringing along, as otherwise it would not be allowed to pass customs. I suppose he thought we might be concealing some blood diamonds or a 1973 copy of the "Miss February" issue of *Playboy* inside one of our cameras. He made it clear that our equipment would be thoroughly inspected upon arrival.

It just got better. The Chairman informed us that our footage would be reviewed by his country's standards and practices board (also known as the Chief Deputy Liaison in Charge of Self Abuse While Viewing Doris Day Films) and that circulation of our production would not be allowed unless any and all suggested changes were implemented.

Upon reading this testimony to the happiest of happy horseshit I went storming into my producer's office.

"Are you kidding me?" I said, tossing the fax on his desk. My producer had no idea what I was talking about, or why I was throwing a piece of paper at him.

"What is it with these guys?" I asked. "Why don't they strap a fucking GPS on us so they can monitor our every step? What do they think we are? Former KGB agents? We don't do approvals, before, during, or after, so this trip is dead before departure. Let's spend our time working on something where they actually get it."

The Chairman and his fellow enforcers didn't have a clue. They could have easily had some invaluable publicity, but we won't shoot content unless we control the final product. It makes no sense for us to act as a production company, which is essentially what The Chairman was insisting we become, when they weren't planning on paying us as such. If a destination wants to own the process and the content, then more power to them. But, they'll have to pay for it. Better yet, they should just crack out their own personal handicams and give it a shot. I'm sure they think it's not that hard—of course, that is, until they actually give it a try.

Once again I remembered my key philosophy. "Don't ask permission, ask for forgiveness." I'd like to explain this to The Chairman, but I doubt if he could ever understand it.

And besides, by now he's probably been "elected" President for Life.

16

Dublin Explosion

With a name like Murphy, it doesn't take a genius to figure out somewhere along the lines I have some acquired some Irish blood. Indeed, my dad's parents were both born in Ireland and eventually immigrated to Chicago, where they raised a family. Everyone wants to explore their roots, so on one of my trips I decided to plan a stopover to do just that.

I was on my way to a conference in Glasgow, Scotland and decided to stop in Ireland along the way. The fact that I had a grandparent born in Ireland gave me something that many outside of the Irish community aren't aware of: the ability to become an Irish citizen while remaining an American citizen by birth. At the time of this trip I had just received my Foreign Births Registry and my Irish citizenship, even though I had never even stepped foot in the country. It was high time I addressed that.

Instead of a connection through London, I flew from the United States directly to Dublin. I went with a buddy of mine, Kevin Phillips, and we decided to explore the city and play a couple of rounds of golf before continuing on to Glasgow later in the week. We would be spending two nights and three days in Dublin, giving us plenty of time to get a taste of the city without having to commit to a more extensive stay.

We rented a car at the airport and headed off to Temple Bar, a happening area in Dublin that is known for its cobblestone streets, boutique hotels, shops, restaurants and pubs. Located between Liffey River to the north, Dame Street to the south, Westmoreland Street to the east and Fishamble Street to the west, this neighborhood was a far different place 200 years ago when it was populated by unsavory characters, various artisans and brothels.

Thanks to years of investment and gentrification, there's now a level of energy that you can feel in Temple Bar, and we were about to immerse ourselves in it. Even though we were tired when we landed, the excitement of a new place had us outside and exploring right after we dropped our bags at the hotel. Dublin is a city of more than a million people, but this neighborhood feels like a small town. We caught plenty of friendly hellos, albeit punctuated with a decidedly Irish accent and accompanied by smiles.

For a big city, Dublin offers a warmth that grows on you quickly, especially on one of those rare sunny days that lifts everyone's mood even higher than usual. I've never been outside the city, but people tell me the hospitality in the small towns and parishes makes you feel like you've been adopted along the way. I've heard stories of dinner invitations and home-cooked meals shared with relative strangers. It's just the Irish way of opening their hearts and homes to the world.

A Night of Guinness and Smoke

We were feeling that Irish magic when later that evening we ventured out with the sister of a colleague we knew back in the States. She lived just outside the city center and had made it a point to come in and spend time with us, and more importantly, drink with us.

In Ireland, one thing you'll do, and do lots of, is drink. Everywhere you turn there is a pub. Almost every block has one. They act as the social hubs for the Irish culture we were about to experience.

There is nothing better than hanging out with locals in any country, and nothing could be much better than doing it in Ireland at a pub. The pub we were in was filled with mostly young Irish people who alternated between sips from their respective pint glasses and drags on their cigarettes. This was all a few years ago, before stricter smoking laws, so the pub was filled with a toxic haze that hung in the air and coated your lungs in tar. I could have done without the smoke, but it did complete the atmosphere. As I looked around it seemed that everybody except me had a cigarette in hand.

Well, what the hell, I thought. This was one of those trips where you couldn't worry about taking care of yourself. Instead it was all about how much fun you could jam into two days.

Even though this was a city pub and our new friend lived outside the limits, she wasn't a stranger here. We immediately connected with her and others, and toasted pint after pint of Guinness Stout. Hey, when in Ireland it doesn't matter what you drink at home. Here, you drink beer. And if you want a taste of the local black gold, that, my friends, is Guinness. So we sat back and downed pint after pint as we laughed while sucking in deep breaths in search of the limited oxygen that remained in the bar. We needed to keep some level of oxygenated blood flowing to our brains.

Despite the fact that we spent an entire evening with her and several others, I couldn't tell you anything more about them than I have already shared. Am I just getting old or is it attributable to the fact that we weren't carrying mobile devices back then and staying connected via Facebook? Maybe, but I chalk it up to the idea that just feeling at home was more important at the time.

Honestly, I wish I could remember even a single name from that night, but alas I'll simply have to reflect on the atmosphere that is created when you hang out with locals in their normal habitat. Each country is different, as are the people you meet, and nothing compares to going local. We did that for this evening, even though my awareness of what was happening around me seemed to fade in and out, no doubt due to the time difference as I figured it. Or maybe the beer.

After several hours of boozing we were about to hit the proverbial wall when a wonderful thing happened: Our jet lag kicked in, making us feel like new men. We caught our second winds and continued to inhale the smoke and the Guinness until the bars closed and the streets grew deserted. Staggering back to the hotel was our next objective, and there we would pass out on our separate twin beds in our very small room. At the time it didn't matter that a few short hours later we would be up and on our way to play our first round of Irish golf.

The Imodium Interrogation

The alarm rang and I remembered the feeling of my tongue smacking the roof of my mouth, except that it didn't' feel like my tongue. At that moment it could have passed for a carpet that an old dog had slept on for the past fifteen years. Every surface of my mouth felt like it had a coating an inch thick on it. That wasn't the only sensation I was feeling at that second. My throat was sore from the smoke and the talk of the night that had ended just a few hours earlier, and my head felt like someone was sitting on it. What a great way to wake up in Dublin!

I rolled over and sent a pillow flying into my roommate Kevin. He stirred, probably feeling the same way I did. I was first in the bathroom and that wasn't good for Kevin, whose dire fate was to use it after I was done. I had barely finished brushing my carpet...I mean my tongue...uh, teeth...when it hit me. I was overcome by a sudden gurgling sensation from somewhere south of my belly button that created a most incredible state of digestive system urgency. I dropped the toothbrush along with my pants and landed hard on the seat.

For the next five minutes I was subjected to the wrenching and purging only a serious night of drinking, or virus, can bring upon your insides. And I thought this happened only in Borneo! Sweat ran off my temples as I finally gathered myself and made it out of the bathroom. Before Kevin even had a chance to get up and take his turn I rushed back inside for another bout.

After a short while I finally felt good enough to get out of the hotel, only to be gripped again on the ride to the course. I needed something as this wasn't going to stop on its own. Can you say Imodium? Indeed, how do you say Imodium in Ireland? I was about to find out.

Kevin was at the wheel and I was on the lookout for what resembled a pharmacy—what they call a chemist. They typically have a small neon sign that looks like a squared-off green cross above their doors. Dead ahead on the right we spotted one and I headed for the curb and some relief.

We were in a residential area of the city, and when I entered the shop it was clear that today was a busy one for getting prescriptions filled. I wasn't sure what to expect when I walked in the door, but it wasn't what I saw. Instead of the typical CVS or Walgreens to which Americans are accustomed, the pharmacies in Dublin are very small affairs with a single counter. There is nothing, at least in this particular pharmacy, that would qualify as self-service. Here you're dealing with the person in the white coat behind the counter, or you're going home empty-handed.

As I waited my turn in a single long line I heard the various requests, questions and follow-up answers that were provided. It seemed that most of those in the crowd at the pharmacy this morning were locals who knew each other and made small talk. Of course, nobody knew me in this place, or even this country, although I could have easily fit in given my heritage. As long as I was quiet I could certainly pass for a local, but that wouldn't last a second after I began to speak.

When I did speak I watched the heads around me turn to locate this "strange" accent as it was decidedly not an Irish brogue. The curious eyes landed on me and the place became utterly silent as I made my request, adding to the discomfort I had been feeling since waking.

Mark: *(leaning in and trying to be quiet)* Uh, do you have something called Imodium?

Pharmacist: Oh, what's that you say?

Mark: I need something we call Imodium. Uh, you know, for diarrhea.

Pharmacist: Sure. I got just what you need.

He turns around and pulls open a drawer behind him and retrieves a box. I shift uncomfortably from foot to foot as I try to keep my eyes down and not get too embarrassed as everyone in the place had no choice but to hear about my personal situation and needs. *In just a few minutes I'll get what I need and this moment will be behind me,* I thought.

Instead of just handing me the box and letting me pay for it, I was subjected to a set of detailed instructions designed, I'm guessing, to make sure I didn't overdose on the stuff. With his hand holding the box up in the air like some kind of prop, the pharmacist began his very detailed explanation of what steps I needed to take with the medicine.

Pharmacist: Aaah, let's see here. Okay, then. Here you have it. You'll need to follow these instructions when taking the medicine. After your first episode you're going to want to take two tablets. That should work and you should be feeling better in no time.

I felt like saying, "Hey buddy, why do you think I'm here? We are well past that 'first episode' marker you're referring to."

Instead I just said "Uh, okay, okay, got it," as I reached out to take the box.

With the slightest move he kept the box just outside of my reach and continued on.

Pharmacist: If you have another episode, after your first episode, then you'll want to take another pill.

Mark: Okay.

Pharmacist: Should you feel the need to take additional doses, do not exceed six in any twenty-four-hour period.

Mark: Right. Can I…

Pharmacist: You should not use Imodium if you have stools that are bloody, black or tarry, or if you have diarrhea that is caused by taking an antibiotic.

At that point I found myself mumbling under my breath something similar to what my father would regularly say when he became exasperated with his seven kids. "Jesus, Mary and Joseph, can I just pay for this and leave?"

Mark: Okay. I'm good.

No wonder the line at the place was so long. This guy was a walking encyclopedia of detailed medical instruction. All I wanted to do was to grab the package, swig a couple of pills with some water *as soon as possible*, and pray that they did the trick. If they didn't, I could say goodbye to the tee time.

With my dignity hanging by a thread I listened to the final instructions, paid and mumbled a "thank you" before heading for the door. The sound in the pharmacy had dropped to almost nothing as the bell on the door announced my departure. I shouldn't have cared that these women were getting a good chuckle at my situation, but I'd be lying if I didn't admit to being very embarrassed. The only saving grace was the thought that this would be the last time any of them would actually see me.

Once back in the car I downed two of the pills and hoped for the best as we made our way to the golf course. I was relieved to have found something that could take care of my current situation and was ready to try my first round of golf in Ireland.

Shock and Awe

As I imagined what the course might look like my vision quickly shifted to what the bathroom at the course might offer first. My stomach was starting to do that thing it did an hour earlier and I knew I was in trouble. A full-on panic was about to set in as I saw the entrance to the course. Phew, now if I can just make it into the clubhouse.

I asked Kevin to drop me at the entrance where I half-waddled, half-walked inside. A crime was about to be committed and I had to figure out where it would ultimately take place, and quickly. I asked directions as I entered and simply barreled down the hall in the direction that was pointed out to me.

One thing about being a friendly nation, as Ireland is, is that it sometimes takes more than a moment to get the information you need. I was relieved to have a quick answer and found myself slamming the door of a stall shut as I swung around to take care of my latest "episode."

Based on what was happening in that stall you could forgive the locals for thinking that there might have been some type of terrorist attack underway. It could have been a biological weapon, or God forbid, a dirty bomb. For all intents and purposes that bathroom was rendered inoperable by any man with the ability to breathe, at least for the next hour or so.

The various exclamations I heard as the door would open, and then suddenly close, were evidence that the damage I had inflicted here would far surpass the damage I would later visit upon the course.

Yeah, I suck at golf. Given a choice between me playing twenty straight rounds and chewing up their course over three weeks, or having another "episode" in their bathroom, I'm confident the members would have chosen the latter.

I ended up destroying their bathroom, as well as some of their lovely fairways, on that first full day in Dublin. If there was good news, at least I didn't do my deeds in front of any of those ladies I saw at the pharmacy.

17

Grand Luxe

Go ahead and admit it. At this point you're a little jealous of these great travel adventures, even those that don't go so well. When I travel I've grown accustomed to nice accommodations and wonderful service in a variety of settings. The fact that we are working while in these places doesn't matter to most people as they think it's all one big holiday. It isn't. The days begin early.

Sometimes the sheer idea of going halfway around the world and being jetlagged for two weeks, away from your loved ones, can be taxing. Add to the fact that the guys I get to hang with don't have much to say and you might even start to feel sorry for me, or not. Most people have a tough time feeling sorry for me because I get to see and do things that some will never have the chance to do. For that I'm very thankful and for that same reason no one wants to hear me bitch.

Well, I'm going to bitch about a trip that sounded great on paper, but was far from it. It was a western rail journey with a company called Grand Luxe, which I mentioned in Chapter 14. The trip we chose was the National Parks of the West on a luxury train that stopped in Santa Fe, Las Vegas, Yellowstone, Grand Canyon, and Jackson Hole, Wyoming.

This sounded like a great trip when we booked it, but it didn't quite turn out that way.

We stayed on the train for the full week and even slept on it. The rooms on the train were tiny, with two twin beds in our case. We also had a tiny private bathroom. During the day the beds would get flipped up and convert to couches.

Even though this was a luxury train, the operators couldn't do much about the underlying track it ran on, which was ridiculously uneven, leading to feelings of being pitched to the ground every so often from the bed. This wasn't the worst part of our nights on board, as the wheels rolling across these old tracks made quite a racket. There were clangs and bangs and squeals to boot. You can create all the luxury appointments you want and still not deliver for things outside of your control. That was the case here.

I had to resort to wearing my Bose headset in an attempt to get any type of shuteye, not that it helped that much. The sounds that still made it through, along with the endless pitching back and forth, made this the longest week without sleep I had endured since I went through "hell week" in my fraternity in the 1980s.

It wasn't all bad, though. During our seven days the trip itself brought us to some wonderful locations, all filled with that stunning western scenery. We really enjoyed the touring aspect of the journey, almost forgetting about our sleep fatigue as we experienced a succession of fabulous mountains, canyons, forests and deserts. The food on board the train and the staff were both outstanding. We just couldn't sleep at night, or at least I couldn't. My son had no problem, as he sleeps like he's dead, but I'm just the opposite. I wake up at the slightest sound or movement, making this the equivalent of the Redeye Express.

Cooked Spam in a Can

Those who could sleep had a really enjoyable trip until we stopped in the rail yard in Las Vegas. It was August, so the temperature outside was around 110 degrees. We ventured off to the Hoover Dam and made it back to the train in the afternoon. While we were gone the train was losing the battle with the sun. Those shiny coaches made of steel and their overworked air conditioners were no match for the summer heat of the Mohave Desert. Imagine stepping from 110 degrees outside to a large tin can that approached the same temperature, but without the benefit of moving air. Can you feel it? We sure did.

A couple of minutes were all we needed to change our mind and head across the parking lot to the Premium Outlets a five-minute walk away. We figured there would be some air conditioning in those stores, hopefully along with one of those misters they have outside to cool people off. With our tongues hanging out and our shoes practically melting on the pavement, we walked toward the buildings that swayed before us. As the heat rose off the payment it distorted the shape of the buildings, making it look more like a mirage than an outdoor mall.

We eventually found ourselves inside one of the stores, hungrily sucking the cool air through our mouths and cursing Mother Nature. At least we were finished filming and didn't have any equipment in tow. That stuff was back on the train getting baked, along with the poor staff that had to stand by until departure time that evening.

Later on, with the red sun falling behind the barren mountain ranges outside of town, our sauna-on-wheels did indeed roll out of the yard, heading north. The staff on board assured us that once we got rolling the air conditioners would kick on at a higher rate and cool us down. We spent our time walking from car to car, hoping to find one that would at least be tolerable while we waited. It was like being in a coed locker room after an intense game of basketball. Sweat was dripping off everyone inside and there was nothing we could do about it. It became a matter of watching the clock and awaiting that magical moment when those air conditioners would be able to overcome the desert.

The temperature eventually returned to something approaching normal, but not till late that night. This was my first experience in mobile heat therapy, and hopefully my last.

When Nature Calls, You Answer

We ventured on to better climates for that time of year, and eventually found ourselves in Zion National Park. This park was a wonderful place to spend the day because you could park your car and hop on the shuttles that could take you to various drop-off points. We picked one that led to a walk into one of the canyons. A nice stream ran alongside the trail and it was absolutely beautiful. The trekking and the water were both great ways to help expend my kids' boundless energy before we headed back to the train.

In the case of Zion, my kids found themselves in the dramatic and shallow Virgin River, splashing around and cooling off. I, on the other hand, found myself wandering and looking for a place to go to the bathroom. You'd think it would be easy to find a spot to go in a national park, especially if you are a guy. All I needed was a tree, but that wasn't as easy as it sounded. The path we chose had plenty of cheerful foot traffic, a river on one side and a steep hill on the other. Getting "lost" to do my business was not the easiest thing in the world. The longer I walked, the more desperate I became. The families that cheerfully said hello as they bounded past me had no idea of the intolerable urgency that was rapidly building within me.

I eventually found a suitable tree away from the constant stream of hikers. I really had to go and actually talked to myself a little bit in the process. I had a hot mike and didn't realize it at the time.

While I was going Nick was listening to every word as he shot B-roll. He picked up everything as clearly as if I was standing next to him. I was cursing and carrying on not only while looking for a spot, but then going in one, so he had a tough time holding the camera steady. Most of what he tried to shoot didn't work out as he kept laughing during my entire experience. That turned out to be a good thing as he wasn't able to use it for an episode of *America's Funniest Home Videos* or some other embarrassing reality show. I don't have to worry about that with Nick, though, as he's as loyal as they come.

So here's a tip that doesn't involve travel: When someone tells you the grass isn't always greener on the other side, it's based on experience. As great as my job is, and as glamorous as it might seem at times, quite often it's the opposite.

It's just my calling. And in this case, nature called, in the middle of nature, and I did my best to answer.

18

The Waffles Made Me Do It!

It started in the tiny dining room of a five-star restaurant in Bruges, Belgium. There were four of us sitting at one of only four tables in this particular area of the restaurant. We were the only ones there. There were two ways into this room: through the open doorway that led to the main part of the restaurant, the way we entered, and a side door that led to a small service bar. Our table was located by the wall where the doors leading to the bar stood.

It was the end of another long day of filming on our eight-day trip to Belgium. We were tired from the nonstop activity and ready for a nice meal. The restaurant wouldn't disappoint, we were sure.

Earlier I had arisen to get in a workout—a standard routine I try to follow no matter where I am. I didn't know it at the time, but it would be one of three workouts that I would experience over the next several hours.

Our shooting concept for the day was to capture the perspective of Bruges from the point of view of a bicycle. Our team suggested that we rent a bike and use a mounted camera to "ride" the viewer all over Bruges. The entire city is a UNESCO World Heritage Site. It's been preserved for centuries and has incredible buildings along cobblestone streets. We figured this "driving tour" might hold some interest for viewers as it switched back and forth between the camera mounted on the bike and another one aimed at me from a van that rolled just ahead.

Have you ever ridden a bike over cobblestones? If so, you will understand that although the historical lanes of Bruges are wonderful to look at and to traverse by foot or by car, they are a very different experience when you're peddling.

Bumpy Ride

We left the hotel, crossed the market square and ended up at the bike rental shop a few doors away. I picked out a sturdy-looking two-wheeler onto which my team mounted the small camera that would capture every twist, turn and bump I would experience. Once it was firmly in place, I set out. Our guide for the day hopped on her own bike and, staying just behind me, gave me instructions on where to go. Step one would be capturing the perspective on the bike as we rolled up and down the streets of Bruges. As I did so our guide acted like my very own personal GPS, making sure that I headed up and down every one of those picturesque streets.

This went on for thirty straight minutes as I heard "turn right," "stay to the left," "just ahead," "turn right at the next windmill..." I followed each and every command and did it at a pretty decent pace. Speed was necessary to smooth out the constant bumps created by the cobblestones and to avoid causing the viewer actual

Beautiful Bruges, Belgium is a UNESCO World Heritage Site.

motion sickness when they watched the edited version. It never became truly smooth on any of those streets, but it was indeed smoother to be moving at a faster pace versus a slower one.

Once my jaunt was completed, we had to repeat the route to capture the rider (that's me) from a moving vehicle just a few yards away. We were counting on our host from Flanders, Geri Jacobs, to drive the van while the guide would provide the turn-by-turn instructions seated in the passenger seat next to her. As Geri drove, her job was to maintain a steady pace up and down the streets. Gene Kang was in the back seat monitoring the sound while Nick Choo sat in the open rear hatch with his Steadicam. We were all set to begin our shoot as I mounted up and took off around the market square. It took a few trips, but we shot the introduction and then headed off to cover the same route I had already done with the camera on the bike.

The pace this time was much slower for a couple of reasons, with the first being that we didn't want to lose Nick out the back of the car. On a couple of occasions we almost did just that as a sudden stop or acceleration had him reaching for something to grab a hold of with one hand while holding the camera steady in the other. It was quite a balancing act and funny to watch from my perspective, although Nick didn't seem to find as much humor in it.

As I rode around on my bike and passed many other bikers, mostly locals, I squirmed on my seat. The forty-five minutes that I had already put into my little riding experience was starting to take its toll on my hindquarters.

Some bicycles have built-in shock absorbers like the ones you see for mountain biking. This feature would have saved me from the

Filming from a moving car provided a great perspective for my bike.

pounding I was taking. In addition to the physical bruising my rear end was taking, my teeth felt like they were chattering. My body was vibrating as the wheels rolled over the cobblestones, mimicking the sound I made as a kid when I hummed with my mouth near a spinning window fan. At a couple of points, I did just that—hummed. It came out as a vibration and it made me smile as it brought back those warm summer nights and oscillating fans of my childhood.

Back in those days nobody had central air conditioning. Heck, you were lucky if you had a window unit. We had one. One. And it was in my parents' bedroom. On a hot summer night growing up as kids you'd see the four youngest Murphys sprawled around the floor as we took shelter from the heat and humidity of a summer night in the northeast. We enjoyed the window unit and its cooling breeze as we drifted off into the night.

Workout Fever

The bumps brought me back to reality and the end of my bike riding adventure. After my ass-Bruging ride around town we shot a couple of additional parts for our segment and called it a wrap. I didn't make it to the gym that day, but I did get a decent bit of exercise in the process of capturing our segment. At dinner later that evening I turned to Gene and asked him how his workouts were coming on this particular trip. They weren't. We had been in Belgium for four nights at this point and Gene had yet to find his way to the gym. On the other hand, I had pushed myself to get up each morning and do something before setting out to film. Hell, I had already banged out several workouts on this trip—if you give me credit for all of that peddling around town, which I think you should!

It wasn't easy keeping that level of discipline, but I'm twenty years Gene's senior and I simply can't go that many days without my workout. I'd either lose my mind and/or gain some serious weight. Neither one was an acceptable option, although some may say the former has already occurred.

It's not always easy to get in a workout in when we travel. Sometimes we are up and out the door quite early to capture a special shot that can be seen only at sunrise, or we end up at a hotel that doesn't have a gym, even if we had time to use one. The excuses can quickly add up so it's important to prepare for any and all situations and get your workout in when the opportunity presents itself.

The challenge in making this happen is the sheer fact that a lot of the world, including Belgium, doesn't believe that much in gyms. When you can find one, it is usually small and, in Belgium, typically empty and not outfitted with the type of equipment most of us crazy American's have come to expect for our routines. That's why I cut Gene a little bit of slack, although that was about to change.

The Joy of Belgian Cuisine

In Belgium they take a different approach to life, one that some would say is healthier. They don't spend hours in the gym on a treadmill to nowhere. Instead, they sit around and drink beer and wine while eating chocolate, waffles and any other delicious thing you can imagine. They eat the best things and don't seem to have the same weight issues that affect so many Americans. A big reason is the fact that Belgians walk everywhere, and I mean everywhere, when you are in Belgium. If you're not walking then you are probably biking. Either way, you're getting a solid dose of exercise each and every day.

The food I ate was not exactly healthy, but it was really tasty and of course, addictive. Who can refuse a single piece of Belgian chocolate or say no to fresh ice cream and chocolate syrup on a warm waffle? Oh, and don't forget to top it all off with some whipped cream for good measure. I figured that consuming any one of these "snacks" would add about 1,500 calories to my daily intake, and that's exactly what I did. I literally ate my way through Belgium. If it wasn't chocolate or waffles it was French fries—all adding up to a much larger me.

Indeed, you'll find French fry stands in the center of Bruges and in shops all over the country. They are part and parcel of the national menu, along with mussels and everything else I mentioned. Another part of the national menu is mayonnaise. Every order of fries comes with a large tub of mayo for dipping. The idea of dipping a fry loaded with fat into an even more fat-filled condiment such as mayonnaise makes my arteries harden just thinking about it.

Sampling beer in Belgium is one of my solemn duties as a travel professional.

The creamy concoctions don't stop there. If you order a cappuccino you might want to make sure it is made with whole milk instead of cream. I can't tell you the last time I had cream with anything, but here it's a staple. If you are used to ordering a skinny latte you can forget about the skinny part, and the Starbucks too, for that matter. I understand that there are only two in the entire country. Indeed, they are as rare as skim milk here.

Despite all of our walking around Belgium I still was putting on weight as we shot some different segments that we thought would interest travelers. One experience we captured involved seeing how beer is made naturally, in part due to yeast that is in the air around Belgium. This is the same way it's been made for hundreds of years, and we visited a working brewery to see just how it's done.

Jet Lag and Grey Goose

But the restaurant I was in that night wasn't about beer. It was five-star all the way, and I was there to have a phenomenal meal in a wonderful setting. It was Geri, Gene, Nick and me, and we discussed what we had accomplished earlier in the day.

At a lull in the conversation, as I mentioned, I turned to Gene and asked him how his workouts were coming that week, already knowing that he had yet to get in even one. There just hadn't been any time unless you were forcing yourself out of bed, with the time change no less, at somewhere around 6:00 a.m. That made it midnight for those of us who live on the eastern seaboard of the United States. That's a tough call with a ten- to twelve-hour day staring you in the face.

I suggested to Gene that he take advantage of the time he had at that moment to drop down and do some pushups.

"No way!" he replied with a laugh.

I tried to get him to do it, but my peer pressure was having no effect. He stuck to his guns. That's when something came over me and I quickly scanned the restaurant to make sure the coast was clear. A moment later, *I* was down on the floor banging out between forty-two and forty-eight pushups. I lost track, but fell short of the fifty I was hoping to do. I popped up, turned to Gene and said, "Your turn."

He shook his head in resignation as if to say, "Shit, now I have to do this…" I ran spotter and made sure the coast was still clear as Gene walked over toward my side of the table. This would put him out of the direct line of sight of the other diners who could see him while he was in his seat.

The next thing we know Gene is on the floor and pumping out fifty pushups as we count along with him. He was about halfway there when I noticed the waiter was headed our way. He mistook my turned head and crazy grin at Gene's move to mean we needed something. I quickly raised my arm and gave him the universal STOP signal with my hand. He held off and Gene completed his task.

As Gene returned to his seat his head moved back and forth as if to say "Did that just happen?" or better yet, "What the heck was I thinking?"

The relative privacy of our little side room made sure our act went unnoticed even though both of our faces were flushed and our heart rates had spiked a bit. As if on cue, the waiter returned to fill our water glasses as we sat there like children who had just gotten away with a bit of mischief that only we knew had happened.

This would be our little secret, the case of the five-star restaurant and the pushups. That is, so far.

Geri, on the other hand, had a complete look of surprise on her face and a genuine smile. I think she thought we were nuts, but I'll just chalk it up to jet lag and…okay…some Grey Goose vodka.

19

What's Up, Doc?

I was on a riverboat on the Mekong River exploring the war-torn country of Cambodia. We were stopping in different villages along the way and seeing just how difficult life is for the Cambodian people, even a decade after the death of Pol Pot and the end of the country's horrendous civil war. This country is exotic and intriguing, though still haunted in ways that may be unexplainable, as I was soon to find out.

The story of Cambodia is a difficult one to fathom, especially in this day and age of immediate news and instant access to information. When you learn the history of what took place as recently as the 1970s you'll be hard pressed to understand how this type of genocide could have taken place in a modern world.

The intellectual capital of the country was virtually wiped out by a campaign to exterminate anyone who was educated. If you had an advanced degree or were a professional you were targeted. Pol Pot wanted to return the country to an agrarian society and those outside that vision had to go.

If you recall the movie *The Killing Fields*, you'll better understand some of the horrors that occurred here. That award-winning film was based on a true story of two journalists trying to escape certain death during Pol Pot's infamous "Year Zero."

One of the strangest experiences I've had while traveling here involved a guy named "Doc." Our ship, the *La Marguerite*, operated by AMAWaterways, had pulled alongside the riverbank and had dropped its gangplank, allowing us access to what looked like a small village. There was no real dock here to accommodate passengers traveling along the river by a luxury vessel like the one we were on, just small access areas for fishermen or small boats.

The contrast between the ship and the countryside was stark. You have well-dressed people on board a small ship that has all the appointments and services of a five-star hotel, yet just a few feet away lies a village that has no paved roads, only muddy ruts where wagons and the occasional motorized vehicle passes.

When we arrived at this particular stop we had no background on what we'd see or do, just our equipment and a healthy curiosity to see what we might discover, as was our usual *modus operandi* with Travel Unscripted. Nick and I walked a few blocks around the town and learned that there was a small market, as well as some ruins that passengers were going to be shown.

The town featured old buildings that didn't seem to include running water or any other type of modern convenience. Garbage was strewn everywhere and puddles of water made for mosquito breeding grounds. This was a rough place to live, and something that's hard to fathom for most people who live in America. It was also hard for us to fathom what we might shoot here.

Good thing for us, the river cruise had a scheduled tour of some ruins that we would be shuttled out to see.

We decided we'd grab our equipment and get shooting. Nick headed back to the ship and I stayed put and took in the scene on the street. I was near a corner that had small open storefronts, if you could call them that. People were sitting inside while kids on bikes road up and down the street. The kids had no shoes on and didn't look like they could afford any even if they wanted to wear them.

Off to my left was a vacant, garbage-strewn lot where another kid was walking and carrying a large plastic garbage bag. It was apparent that he was picking up bottles, just like so many homeless people in the States.

The Weirdness of Shared History
(or, It's a Small World)

I was lost in my thoughts when I heard a voice off to my right, a distinctly American voice. "See that kid right there?" the voice said. "If he was in the States he'd be the best pitcher on his team. You should see him throw a ball. That kid over there, he is super-fast. You should see him run."

Huh? I turned my head and saw a rather grizzled man who looked like he might not be that old, maybe in his late forties, but definitely had done some hard living. His face was rough and creased with wrinkles, with a growth of white beard. His clothes were slightly dirty, he was gaunt and his teeth had seen better days. This guy could end up working as a Keith Richards impersonator, but maybe not here in Cambodia.

Our eyes met. "You're obviously American. What are you doing here in Cambodia?" I ventured.

"I came here seven years ago and never left."

My next question had to do with what he might do in a country like Cambodia and the answer surprised me. "I'm a photo-journalist and I travel around and shoot photos as part of a cooperative."

He asked me what I did and I told him that we worked with a travel media company and were here to shoot video. As soon as I spoke those words, this guy seemed to change before my eyes. He straightened up. His gaze sharpened on mine and he almost seemed like a different person in some unexplainable way.

He asked me if I had ever heard of a magazine called *Travel Weekly*.

"Sure I have," I sputtered as my jaw dropped. For a number of years this magazine had competed with one that I ran, and competed for a while with my own company that I started in 2002.

Here's how the rest of the conversation went:

I worked there on a product called Jaguar. You know it?" he asked.

"Know It? I actually interviewed for a job on it back in 1990." Jaguar was a hotel directory on a CD-ROM, and back in those pre-Internet days, it was expected to be a very big deal—a cutting-edge media project. I had turned down an offer to work on it and instead went to a traditional travel trade magazine.

I would have taken that job with Jaguar if not for one key person: the guy who ultimately became my mentor of sorts, John Ballantyne! He was running Jaguar just before I went in for my first interview, but had moved over to the magazine that I eventually joined. He had an inside track on the candidates the Jaguar people were interviewing. As soon as they offered me a sales job, his "mole" picked up the phone, gave John a heads-up, and *he* hired me.

The call came from the recruiter, who assured me it was unusual. The recruiter knew that John was a *former* client and was asking specifically for me to come in for an interview at his new gig, even though the recruiting firm was supposed to be working for Jaguar.

It is highly unorthodox, some might say unethical, for a placement firm to do something like this. It effectively meant that all of the work that their client had done to select me for a position was wiped out when I was offered a job elsewhere. For me, however, it was a blessing as I was much better suited to be in the environment I chose, rather than the one where the sun-baked guy standing before me had worked.

Besides the fact that Doc worked at Jaguar, and might have been my colleague at some point had I gone that route, there was another surprise. The person who took the job that I turned down was a woman named Cheryl Scheideler.

Doc asked me if I happened to know Cheryl while we were standing on that dirty street corner. I smiled and said, "Do I know her? I went to grade school with her!"

Doc's eyes bulged out of his head with this statement and looked on in complete disbelief. I assured him that this was indeed the truth and he told me that I had to tell Cheryl what he was up to. Doc wanted to make sure that Cheryl knew he was "okay" and that he was "going to die here in Cambodia."

Sure Doc, whatever you say, I thought. *We all have to go sometime, and you being a Doc and all might give you some insight into the day and time of your demise. I'll just have to continue plodding along until the mighty hand of God comes down and takes me away. Until then, I'm just going to keep on seeing the world, shooting my videos and writing my stories.*

So, as Doc stood there I decided to use my iPhone and shoot a short video that I could send to my high school friend—right from the streets of Cambodia! I was able to send it straight to her inbox, delivering one of the most "out there" surprises of her life. Ain't technology wonderful?

This whole little episode from a dusty village in one of the most haunted places on Earth illuminates one of those universal truths. It shows that despite all of the wonders of the modern-day world, including instant videos from the farthest corners of the globe—it's those surprising serendipities of life that involve people, the timeless dynamic of human interactions with paths unexpectedly and delightedly crossed, that can be the most mind-blowing experiences of all.

20

Cooking with Cookie Monster

The all-inclusive resort is a great way to vacation with the family, as there are plenty of structured activities for the little ones, with minimal chance of busting your wallet on "extras" and other unexpected expenditures. One such resort that I really like is Beaches. This brand is an offshoot of the Sandals Resort business, arguably the biggest player in the Caribbean resort business. For your sake, let's hope that if you visit this wonderful place your good times are not invaded by a strangely dressed man standing near your kids.

Yes, that was me, but hold on...I can explain.

A few years ago my company was hired to visit and film each of their properties. It put me on the road for almost three straight weeks, but I did get to stay at several of the properties while taking care of the video shoots, including their three Beaches resorts at the time. They had two in Jamaica—one in Ocho Rios and the other in Negril. We spent time at both of these properties and I brought my family along for the experience. (They also have a Beaches property at Turks and Caicos.)

Nick and I were considering how we'd shoot each of these resorts uniquely in order to keep the various segments interesting. One of the best ways we've found to do this is to focus on the experiences you can have when you travel. One of the special experiences they created at Beaches has to do with Sesame Street. Several years ago they signed a deal to have their characters on location and to create activities that included them.

This partnership puts Sesame Street branding and their characters all over the resort. Kids go crazy as they interact at different times and in different places with the likes of Burt and Ernie, as well as Elmo.

Being a father I was very familiar with Sesame Street, and in particular Elmo. My son's voice for most of his early years had a strange resemblance to Elmo. Indeed, that's what most of my family members called him. By the time we ended up at Beaches that day he was well beyond the age of the typical Sesame Street viewer, but he still enjoyed seeing the characters as they showed up in different spots. I think the adults also enjoyed it, to be frank. It brought back memories of either our own childhoods or reminded us of our own children when they were little. Either way, it's a great addition to the resort concept.

The kids' camp at the property featured the larger-than-life characters at different points throughout the day, but there were also some fun scheduled activities that you could take advantage of. One of those activities was called Cooking with Cooking Monster. We thought it might be fun to include this as part of our segment, keeping in tune with the idea of showcasing experiences.

Questionable in a Chef's Hat

We set up to shoot ahead of the arrival of Cookie, with the idea of me jumping in and interacting with him. This was during his regu-larly scheduled activity for all kids on property so I found myself standing around with an assortment of youngsters ranging from just over a year to eight or nine years of age. Some of the kids had their parents there, ready with their digital cameras and camcorders to capture the moment. Some parents opted to drop their kids with the camp counselors and enjoy the serenity while the resort shuttled the kids to the different activities including this one.

Everyone got a chef's hat and apron and waited eagerly for Cookie to appear. We were there to cook with Cookie so we had to look the part! I donned similar props, standing there with the kids, the counselors and a handful of adults. The counsel-ors were young adults, and the kids were kids. The parents who stuck around were interacting with their little ones. Everything

Would you let your kids near the guy on the left?

213

looked completely normal and part of a picture except for one thing; the forty-something guy wearing a chef's hat and apron waiting patiently to "Cook with Cookie Monster." It didn't take long for me to notice a number of strange sideways glances coming from one mother in particular.

Here's the problem: It was obvious that I wasn't there with any kid in particular. I was standing by myself because Nick had taken the opportunity to grab a seat about thirty feet away from where I stood. I had no idea at the time, but the mother staring at me must have thought I was Mr. Creepy or something. That's what a friend of mine told me when I related the story. She said that when she is out with her small children she cautiously scans the surrounding area for those people who seem to be out of place. She thought this lady was probably doing the same thing and had already identified me as a potential threat to her kids.

Maybe that's why she turned to me and said, with what might have been a slight hint at sarcasm, "Wow, you must be a huge fan."

"Excuse me?" I replied. I had no idea at that moment what she was referring to.

She looked at me with one of those forced smiles. "Of Cookie Monster. It looks like you are going to be cooking with him so I assume you must be a big fan." Or put another way it was if she was saying "Hey, freak, what's with playing with furry kid characters?"

It took me a moment to process what she was saying and I started to laugh. You know the kind of laugh I'm talking about. As I tried to explain that I was there to work it didn't quite come out right. I finally resorted to pointing to Nick and made a motion like a camera rolling to get my point across. I wanted to make sure that she knew I was there working and not some social misfit... or even something worse.

It took her a moment to put two and two together and in that time frame she became a different person. She relaxed and smiled, a real one this time—the kind of relaxed smile you should have on vacation.

"Oh my God," she said, "I couldn't figure out what you were doing here. It looked really strange!"

I was able to clearly talk at this point and told her what we were up to.

"Too funny. Well, don't worry. I'm not a pedophile. Just a dad who gets to bring his wife and kids on a trip like this while I do some work."

She nodded and laughed...but was that a real laugh? Did she believe my story? Maybe I'll never really know, because even though Nick then came over with the camera equipment and more or less introduced himself, he didn't really help matters. True to form, he only muttered a few somewhat incomprehensible words, and honestly, I'm not sure that did the trick. For all she knew, we could have been tag-team pedophiles.

Moral of the story: If you're a guy and going to be around a gathering of kids, don't show up alone dressed as an outlandish chef. It may help you meet females, but not in the way you want.

21

The Joy of Family Vacations

Family vacations are one of the greatest ways to spend time with your loved ones. The strains of work, school and kids' activities all disappear when you get away and have nothing to think about other than having some family fun. Just watch your skin… and your wallet.

You can create a great family vacation in a number of different ways. There are different types of vacations depending on the age of the kids, the activities everyone is interested in and your budget. Where I live in New Jersey puts us forty-five minutes away from the shore, and that's a big draw for families. Indeed, many of the families in our area have invested in shore homes where they spend the better part of their summers, as well as long weekends.

Those who don't have an actual shore home have the option of renting. Weekly rentals are very common and range from $1,500 for a week in a condo to several thousand dollars for a four-bedroom home on a beach block. Opt for the biggest and the best and you could be looking at significantly more for that one-week getaway.

Even though lots of people love their beach houses, don't count me in that camp. I think they are nuts for a number of reasons, especially if they are descended from the Irish or English. At the beach, you can't miss these pasty white people—so bright they seem to glow. I guess they don't see much of the sun, so when it finally comes out they welcome it with open arms, only to end up with a burn that makes the people who see it cringe. You see these people with their painful burns and can only wonder what they were thinking throughout the day. Some will tell you they are working on their base, but the base of what—a future freckle patch?

I can speak from experience because I'm half Irish and have never been known to tan. That didn't stop me from having similar experiences as a kid when parents weren't aware of the concept of sunblock or SPF. My brothers and sisters would leave the house in the morning and not return till after sundown, sun protection be damned. My parents either didn't know or simply didn't care about the dangers of the sun back then. I chalk it up to ignorance of the risk, as this was the same generation raised on the idea that cigarettes were actually good for you, not something that would lead to your early death.

Besides the future prospects of skin cancer that people like me are courting when hanging out on a beach, I'm not a fan of the whole rental market for another reason. When I'm on vacation, I don't want to be doing laundry, washing dishes, or cooking meals. I don't mind toasting up some bread, mixing up some hot chocolate or pouring some cereal for my kids, but that's as far as I'm willing to go.

Family vacations on Lake Michigan, sun protection be damned.

If I choose a condo-style property it needs to be one that has all of the related hotel services included. I'm not willing to forego the housekeeping and other benefits for a refrigerator and mini stove. The nice condo hotels represent the best of both worlds, but aren't always available in many of the destinations you might be considering for a vacation.

There's another reason why I'm not a big fan of the Jersey Shore idea for a vacation not even counting the "do it yourself" nature of this type of travel. It's not as cheap as you might think. When people factor in the cost of the rental and the other costs for dining out, assuming they want to have some downtime and simply relax, it can really add up. What starts out looking like a real value will run into the thousands of dollars for that single week.

I don't want to appear like I'm dissing the whole Jersey Shore thing, as Snookie and her friends might take issue with it. That crowd does the whole summer house rental thing, but I wouldn't call it a vacation by any means. It's more like a place to hang out and drink with friends than anything else. This works when you're young, single and don't have kids. You should actually like sand, too, which isn't really my thing.

I'll stick to seeing the world through the eyes of the people I meet.

The Shore Alternative for Vacations: Cruising

Okay...then what should you consider if you have kids and want to go on vacation? You've got several great options depending on your interests, budget and where you live in the country.

For example, almost seventy percent of the U.S. population is within a three-hour drive of a cruise ship. From where I live, I can drive to ports in New Jersey, New York or Baltimore and board a ship that takes me to the Caribbean in roughly one and a half days. Because I'm driving, and not flying, I can save on the headaches, the hassles and the costs of flying with kids. I can allocate those costs to other things such as excursions or drinks while on board, as they have separate costs over and above the cost of the cruise itself, in most cases.

Cruises marketed as "all inclusive" include many things you get as part of the overall price when you book it. They are a great value, but you need to be aware that you will still incur additional costs. Starbucks is on board Royal Caribbean's new *Allure of the Seas* ship, but you'll pay for each latte or frappuccino you order. Want a mojito at their Cuban-themed bar and you'll pay for that as well. Go outside of their standard dining options and you'll pay an up charge for that finer dining.

It's one of the ways the cruise lines can offer some very attractive pricing at the point of purchase yet still make a handsome profit. Things like soda don't come free, and we all know how much soda kids drink. They offer soda passes that can be purchased at the start of the trip for an unlimited supply of soft drinks. I'd recommend this option, as you'll quickly surpass this package price if your kids are apt to digest the sugary stuff.

You also want to be careful if your kids like to play arcade games as this too can do some serious damage to your budget. My son spent fifty dollars in less than an hour in the arcade of one of these ships. That was his budget for the entire trip so he didn't spend much more time there after that.

Instead, he had a blast with the many free activities that are available on today's large cruise ships. For example, you'll find rock walls that can be climbed, zip lines, water slides, miniature golf, ice skating rinks, movie characters and more. They are all designed to appeal to families, especially multi-generational ones. There is literally something for everyone, including quiet, adults-only spaces if you aren't interested in hearing a bunch of screaming kids. My son could have been happy with only one feature on his first of many cruises; an elevator! This kid literally rode the elevators up and down at every chance, staring out through the glass at the large atrium below. Indeed, when he "disappeared" we simply went to the main elevator banks and, presto, there he was!

The key to value-packed cruising is to watch those additional costs that go beyond the free elevator rides. For those who are good at budgeting themselves and watching what they spend, this isn't an issue. For those who are less inclined or simply want to know their entire cost up front, I'd suggest looking for a land based all-inclusive resort that caters to families.

It's also important to do some comparative shopping with the assistance of a travel professional, because there is no "one

I always enjoyed visiting the Philadelphia Zoo with my mom.

size fits all" solution for families. Do you think that one cruise line is going to direct you to another, even if it is a better fit for you and your family? Not a chance. You'll find different levels of service and product out there and sometimes it's hard to understand where the best value meets the best experience for you. Perhaps you've heard the old tale about the magician who was working on a cruise ship for the disreputable and fictional budget line "Cruise-Mart." In this case there was a different audience each week for the cheesy magic show, so the magician allowed himself to do the same tricks over and over again.

There was only one problem: the magician's recently acquired parrot saw the shows each week and, being pretty smart animals, began to figure out the secret of every trick. Once he understood he started shouting in the middle of the show: "Look, it's not the same hat!" "Look, he is hiding the flowers under the table!" or "Hey, why are all these cards the Ace of Spades?"

After a while, the magician became furious. The cruise director for this el-cheapo outfit wasn't so happy about the situation either, and finally disposed of the magician and parrot by putting them on a tiny launch and pointing them in the general direction of a nearby group of islands. For the first day the magician and the parrot just stared at each other with hate, but did not utter a word. The ice was finally broken when the parrot finally spoke, uttering "Okay, I give up. Where's the ship?"

Trust me, you don't want to be on that kind of line, or even in that sort of resort, so stick with the better brands and avail yourself of the travel pro's expertise. The travel providers pay the agent's commission so it won't cost you a thing. Remember that there's really no such thing as a free midnight buffet! You're paying for it one way or the other, so find the right fit for your family.

My mom and me. The nut with the tank is my older brother Tom.

22

First-Class Germs

I get to go all over the world as part of my job, experiencing new destinations and visiting some old familiar ones. Most of the time it is truly fantastic, and I understand that most people would kill to be able to do what I do. I'm always getting offers to take people with me who say that they can "carry my water" or run one of our cameras. However, you should know that my job can be highly hazardous at times. Disease can rear its ugly head at any time, and I'm not talking about malarial situations in third-world cesspools. Sometimes it can strike in first class—in Seat 1B to be precise.

Here's the truth about traveling for a living: What looks like a ton of fun is truly hard work. When we are on location, we are focused on the job at hand—that is, getting the right shots and putting together the story lines that will make our content interesting and fun to watch. That doesn't leave a lot of free time to simply kick back and enjoy a particular place like most tourists.

Sure, I get to see and hear plenty of amazing things, but generally I'm not going to sit down at some café, grab a glass of wine and just enjoy the scene in front of me as if I were on vacation. More likely, we are carrying equipment across the market square, bypassing those beautiful cafés on our way to shoot some cathedral or other location. If we stop to grab a drink, it's typically a hurried process that leaves a bit to be desired. What's more, our drinks mostly revolve around caffeine, as we might be dragging some serious ass at any given time.

One of the only times you can really relax is on the plane either coming or going. If we are going, then we are usually on a red-eye flight, especially for most international travel, and we need to get some sleep. We don't want to waste any days so we might fly to Europe at night, catch a few hours in our seats, then land and shoot. It's more likely that we get a chance to chill out on the way back after a successful trip.

On a recent trip to Jamaica I was lucky enough to get my complimentary upgrade to first class for both the originating and return legs. I boarded in Philadelphia for the three-hour nonstop flight to Montego Bay and was getting ready to sit down when the man in the window seat next to me asked if I'd mind switching with his wife. He pointed to the second row window seat where she was sitting.

A little background here: When you fly as much as I do you get that coveted loyalty status with the airline. In my case, I'm a "Chairman's Preferred" member on US Airways, the main carrier out of my closest international airport in Philadelphia. This status means that I get automatic upgrades to first class when they are available. It also means that the airline tries to give me my preferred seat when it's available. I'm also guaranteed a seat on a booked flight, even if it's oversold, while they bump someone else who doesn't fly quite as often.

The reason this is valuable to me is simple: economics. Unlike the casual leisure traveler who is very price-focused with plenty of lead time, travelers like me often have to book at the last minute. What that means is that I have to pay a significant price premium as compared to my leisure friends on board. For instance, my last-minute ticket to Jamaica was over $1,000 for economy. Had I booked that same exact flight a few weeks earlier, the price would have been less than $500. And that's why these airlines go out of their way to make people like me happier than the general population. We drive a huge chunk of their revenues as we typically fly each and every week, often at the last minute, and at a big premium.

So, when people on a plane ask me to switch seats before I've even put my luggage up, like this guy in 1A did, I'm open to the request. I'm generally down with the switch as long as it's to a seat that is similar to the one I'm assigned, like one bulkhead aisle for another. I think most people are the same way. It's a far different situation when I'm asked to give up my seat for something that is far less desirable. For instance, a seat that has someone in front of you reclining into your lap. Still, I always do my best to find a solution when people ask to be united with their loved one on a flight.

In this case, when the guy in 1A asked me to switch with his wife, I looked over and saw that she was sitting in 2A, a window seat that would have the exact scenario I hate.

"Uh, no…sorry, but I don't like the window seat."

He frowns. I try an idea that might get them what they need.

I look at the guy in 2C, right next to the wife, and say "Hey would you want to sit over here in the bulkhead window so these two can sit together?"

"No, I don't like window seats," he responds, something I totally get.

I then follow up by saying "Why don't you take my aisle seat then, and I'll jump in the bulkhead window."

"Sorry, but I need to be able to put my bag under the seat in front of me..." Granted, you can't do that in a bulkhead, but I thought that was a pretty lame excuse. It's simple enough to put it in the overhead and take it down right after takeoff.

Well, you can't say I didn't try. I really did, but there were no takers. I didn't stop with the first "no" or even the second one. It didn't matter. The husband who was watching this exchange developed what could only be described as an angry pout. The guy was genuinely pissed off when he didn't get his way. He suddenly stopped looking like an adult and morphed into the spoiled little kid that he once was. I didn't get so much as a "thanks for trying" from the guy, but I did get one from the wife. I'm guessing the guy is the high-maintenance moody bitch in that partnership.

For the rest of the flight he didn't utter a sound, and I was happy for the silence. In fact, his wife should have slipped me a few bucks at the end of the journey for giving her a break from him. What a jerk. He sat and pouted next to me for the entire flight, not able to even make eye contact. It didn't matter that I tried to help them out. He was just an angry man.

This incident gave me an idea for a new TSA screening concept. They could create a jerk screener or something like that to identify people like this one when you travel. You can then change their seats to make sure that they all get to sit together and enjoy each other's company! How great would that be? They deserve each other, at least for a few hours.

Waiting for God's Shuttle

My stay at Sandals was much better than my experience on the flight down, thank goodness. It's always great to be on location at a beautiful resort; the air travel is simply what we suffer through to make it to paradise. However, paradise didn't last long for me on this jaunt, as I had only two nights to actually enjoy it.

I made the return trek to the Montego Bay airport for my 2:00 p.m. flight home. I was waiting in the first-class line at the check-in counter, a little perk that fliers with "status" can use to escape the long economy lines that tend to snake around the waiting area and move like snails, especially in places like Jamaica. Those tedious lines are something that airlines should work on, as they really can ruin the afterglow of a great, relaxing vacation.

At least I didn't have to deal with a long line on this particular flight, and I figured that I'd be cruising through Jamaican immigration in a matter of minutes. It didn't quite work out that way as the two people in front of me appeared to have some issues. They were both elderly and sitting in wheelchairs. The husband was hooked up to one of those oxygen tanks for people suffering from respiratory diseases like emphysema. The check-in process needed to verify the manufacturer of the oxygen, as well as other particulars, to make sure the tank wouldn't create a hazard when in flight.

That was okay with me. The airline has to know these things because some products can react a wee bit negatively in a pressurized cabin when a plane is whizzing around at 32,000 feet above the earth. The last thing you need is for an oxygen tank to pop.

I'd rather stand around and be bored for a bit waiting for these issues to be addressed versus getting blown out of the sky when something goes wrong. That's why I never understand people who get pissed off when a flight gets canceled or delayed due to a mechanical issue. It sucks, and it is very disruptive for people trying to get to a cruise ship or make a connection, but what can the airline do about it? Take off and "hope for the best"? I don't think so. When I see and hear the bitching I feel like going up to these people and asking them if they'd prefer the alternative: a rapid descent into the Earth.

While everything is getting sorted out in front of me, I finally got the wave to head to a different counter. Once again, the "status" was paying off as they ignored the next economy passenger and invited me to check in via that line. I turned to grab my roll-on bag and I realized that I was surrounded by a contingent of the infirm. I had two wheelchair-bound seniors in front of me and one behind me. I was starting to think I was going to be flying on "God's Shuttle" instead of US Airways. Hey, it was lucky for this entourage that they made it through their vacation. I've heard stories of how some in this age group make the return trip in the cargo area, if you know what I mean.

I finally got checked in and headed through immigration. An hour later I boarded the flight and noticed that the guy sitting in the seat next to mine was the same person who rolled up in the wheelchair behind me at the ticket counter. He had to be late sixties, or older, overweight and moving slowly. In other words, he wasn't exactly a picture of health. As these thoughts were going through my mind, I heard the couple in the row behind us say, "We really loved Sandals…!"

Huh? I look at them and didn't really understand why they were directing this statement at me. What I didn't immediately remember was that I was wearing a Sandals polo shirt that was a gift from the resort owner, Gordon "Butch" Stewart. I had spent the last two days with Butch and members of his team, and had experienced two of his properties in the process.

The wife pointed the shirt out to me and I had one of those Charlie Sheen moments. *Duh, Sandals shirt, dude!*

I immediately asked them a bunch of probing questions and learned that they had just taken their first trip to Jamaica and stayed at their first Sandals resort. They loved both the country and the resort, they were on their twentieth anniversary and so on. I gathered this information quickly and shared some of my own. I can't tell you how many times, but suffice it to say I've probably been to Jamaica between twenty-five and thirty times in the past two decades. I've simply lost track of all of the trips. In one year alone I can remember traveling there five times, all for business.

Sex for Hire, Ominous Hacking and Other Delights

As I was sharing this tidbit to the amazement of my new friends, the heavy, wheezing guy in the seat next to me, you know, the guy in the chair at check-in said "I've got you beat. I've been here close to fifty times."

"You win," I said, and I meant it. That's a lot of travel to a single island.

"What brings you down here so much, work?" I asked.

"I just like it here..."

That was the beginning of one of the more interesting flights I've been on in my past two decades of travel. This guy—I'll call him "Chuck"—and I talked about Jamaica, politics in the United

States, our wives and more. I shared some of the stories of my travel adventures in Southeast Asia and he told me about his business and some of the horrors he's experienced in that regard.

As it turns out he's a consultant who works with both insurance companies and individuals, many of whom have been severely injured in the line of work. In one story he shared, a crane operator got too close to a power line and the resulting arc of electricity fried his arms and legs, leaving him as a quadriplegic. It wasn't exactly an uplifting conversation at this point, as he explained what this poor guy was suffering through financially as well as physically. In fact, it was downright depressing.

Things turned a little bit more positive, and interesting, when he mentioned his Jamaican girlfriend. That caught me off guard as I could have sworn he also told me about his wife who had a condition that didn't allow her to travel.

"Hold on a sec…didn't you say you were married?" I asked.

"I am, but I have this girl I've been seeing in Jamaica for the past two years"

All I can think is this. "Who the hell is doing this guy?" No offense to my older friends, but it turned out that he was sixty-four but looked a good decade older. After all, he was obese and had a difficult time getting around. Hello! Can you say wheelchair while waiting to check in!

And this guy has a girlfriend? Okay, next question up. "How old is she?"

"I have to tell you, I'm going to hell for this," he states. "She's twenty-eight." He adds, "She looks like a model, but Jamaica is so poor that I'm helping her with some money and it's working out for both of us..."

I tried to keep my mind away from the vision of these two alone together. I didn't want to go there under any circumstances.

I ask, "How's it working out at home?"

He responds with "Not so great. She keeps asking for more and more money every time I'm there."

What I actually meant with the question, of course, was how it was working out with having a wife and girlfriend duo, not how it's working with the girlfriend and the money!

"Oh, she doesn't know anything about the girlfriend. She actually thinks I have a gay lover named Tom down here."

What? As this conversation is taking place, and my new friend isn't a quiet talker, I imagine the thoughts running through our fellow travelers' minds. What could they actually be thinking? I know what I was thinking. *This is crazy!*

Something else was going on at the same time I was listening to my seatmate's personal life. He was hacking and coughing every few minutes. For those who know me, I'm a bit neurotic about germs. That is in part due to my endless travels. The last thing I need to do is get sick, as it completely screws with my schedule, resulting in a domino effect of cancellations. One of the best ways to avoid this is to avoid people who are hacking up fur balls on the plane next to you, but where to go? No empty seats existed around me and you can wash your hands only so many times.

I made it a point not to touch the center console between the two seats, leaving me about twelve inches of space to work with. The reason for this was quite simple. I'd watch his hands move from his mouth to the armrest to his mouth again, over and over. Each time he covered his mouth to cough, I imagined more and more mindless, wriggling germs going from that hand to that armrest and the seat in which he sat.

I figured I was okay as long as I kept my hands to myself. That wasn't going to be an issue because my hands didn't leave my lap, but "Chuck" was a touchy guy. As he made a point or simply had something new to add he would reach over and give me one of those arm taps. The kind that isn't too annoying in its own right, but becomes disconcerting when the arm touching you is potentially carrying God-only-knows what kind of cough-hacking germs.

As I learned more about his girlfriend, and his descriptions shifted from that term to his "whore," I decided I could use a long, hot shower to wash this mess away from me, body and soul. That wasn't going to happen, so I took the opportunity to disengage, use the bathroom, and wash my hands for the umpteenth time.

When I opened the door to the bathroom I noticed that Chuck was out of his seat grabbing something from the overhead bin. I stood off to the side, just in front of the galley, and waited for him to finish. I figured he'd be making his way back into his window seat. I could have sat down as there was plenty of room for him to slip by—one of the reasons I like bulkhead seats—but I stood to give him a little extra room to make his way back. He wasn't exactly moving quickly or easily so it would certainly make it easier if I stayed standing.

Unfortunately, things weren't exactly going right for me that day. At that point Chuck asked if he could switch seats with me for the rest of the flight. I immediately froze as a vision of sinking into a warm soft hole full of cooties overtook my mind. I banished that thought and told Chuck that I was fine and that he could simply take his time. I'd wait for him. As they say in Jamaica, "Hey, no problem Mon!"

"I'd really appreciate it if you could switch because I'm going to be a bit"

"I'm good. I could use a stretch," I replied. I then bent over at my waist to theatrically stretch my low back and hamstrings, as if to emphasize the point.

"It's tough for me to get up and down from in there and I'll need to do it a few more times…if you could switch…?" He asked again.

"No problem, Chuck," I said, but didn't really think. I was about to sink into the germ equivalent of a black hole, maybe to never return again! Okay, maybe that's a little dramatic, but I was beyond disgusted as I slid in and sunk into the seat that Chuck had left nice and warm for me. I mean, really nice and warm. He must have been running a fever as it felt like one of those seat warmers you have in your car. That initial feeling was gross, but it was about to get worse.

Before I even had a chance to grab my computer, iPad, head-phones or magazines from the accompanying seat, Chuck was busily rubbing his puffy hands all over them.

"Here, I got that for you…" as he picked up and handed me one thing after another.

"That's it, I'm surrounded," I thought. There was no doubt in my mind that I had just dramatically increased my chance of catching, at best, a nice cough or cold, or something far worse if luck would have it.

A Good Game of Twister, Followed by Decontamination

The banter continued for the final hour of the flight with me doing my best to not touch my face with my hands. Any doctor will tell you that this is the way most people get sick. They touch a germy surface and then transfer that little contamination to nose or mouth.

What happens when your nose itches in this situation? My hands and arms were bare because I was wearing a polo shirt, meaning that I wasn't comfortable addressing an itchy eye or nose with my forearm. I felt compelled to try to use my shoulder to accomplish that task.

At this point, I'd ask you to stop reading for a moment and see if you can rub your nose with your shoulder, or better yet, try rubbing your eye.

Go ahead, try it. It's not easy, and that's what I was learning very quickly. Not a fun feeling when you forget to take your allergy medicine that day. On top of the feeling, I actually looked ridiculous in the process. Good thing nobody was there to witness it other than Chuck.

Finally, after what seemed an eternity, the flight landed in Philadelphia and I prepared to get up and grab my roll-on and briefcase from the overhead. I normally use both hands to accomplish this, with one on the handle and the other balancing the particular bag. That option was out as Charlie reached out with his germ infested mitt to give me a nice firm handshake and to thank me for a good flight.

My hand immediately became quarantined as it came into direct contact with the same hand that Charlie had been using every time he coughed. Indeed, just moments before reaching out to shake my hand that same hand was catching the spittle coming from his mouth as he hacked for about the fiftieth time in three hours.

What happened next made me look like a stroke victim. I started to reach out to remove my luggage, but I was only using my left arm. There was no way that right hand was going to come into contact with any items that couldn't be immediately washed at the sign of the first restroom. So as I'm swinging one bag after the other out, trying not to take someone's head off as it drops to the floor, I've got this crazy grin on my face.

"Am I neurotic or what?" I think. There was no stopping me at this point. I was first off the plane, hauling my bags in my "good hand. "I made a beeline to the nearest sink available. Then, with the full, horrific knowledge that my arms had been all over his seat and armrests, and not just my hands, I placed my hand inside the lower portion of my polo shirt to unclasp my watch, once again protecting any physical belongings.

This was going to be a complete scrub, something you see on those medical shows as the surgeons prepare to operate. With both arms free and a hands-free faucet, I covered my skin in water and began the decontamination process. First my right hand and arm all the way to my bicep, followed by my left arm. A quick rinse and dry, and I was on my way, fingers crossed.

So how would it turn out? Did I succeed in my efforts to remain cold-free? Nope. Two days later good old Chuck reared his head again as I woke up with a sore throat.

An ounce (or in this case, a couple of gallons) of prevention didn't quite cut it in this scenario. Yes, flying can be hazardous, even in first class.

23

The Cleanest Bums in the World

The Japanese make great cars as anyone who has ever driven one knows. They also lead the world in electronics with brands such as Sony, Mitsubishi and Hitachi. As great as these marvels are, I've found something in my travels to Japan that has them all beat: their toilets. That's right, their toilets are engineering marvels that have the ability to do many interesting things all at the touch of a button.

Have you ever seen a toilet with a control panel? How about one with a user guide? Well, you have both in Japan. How about a seat that senses you are standing in front of it, then automatically rises so you don't have to reach down and lift it up? This is important if you are a man, and even more important for the women who use the facilities after we do. Japanese toilets have these features and more.

Imagine it's the middle of the night and you feel the call of nature. You get up and wander to the bathroom in the dark and cold. You ease your butt down, and instead of a cold seat that initially shocks, you are greeted by a seat that is several degrees warmer than your body making you think "Aaaaghhhhh...that's nice." Every time you sit down on it you have similar thoughts. It never gets old.

Which brings up another issue. We guys don't take full advantage of these toilet contraptions, because we stand more often than not when going, so should we be sitting more often so we can get our money's worth on these investments?

Well, how many guys do you know who sit when they go number one? Not too many in my book, but there is this one guy at work. Yep, he's actually made it clear that this is his style of going. I'm not sure why he has shared this somewhat intimate detail, but indeed he has. There are some things you need to keep to yourself and this goes down as one of them. Because he has spent significant time in Japan, I'm wondering if he became addicted to squatting as a result of the heated seats he may have experienced. I guess anything is possible, but I will leave it to his memoirs to share the shocking reality.

For most of the rest of us guys, standing to take care of business amounts to a big plus, especially when you have to use public facilities. That habit could quite possibly change if and when you pick up a couple of these high-tech Japanese toilets and have them shipped to your house. They aren't cheap, though, as you'll see if you search for one online. If you go for the entire unit, including the bowl and tank, some models will set you back more than $5,000. I've been told that you can go up to $25,000 for one of them. That's ridiculous, but there must be a market for them somewhere. That's a luxury item if there ever was one. If you're looking to install one over your existing toilet you can do the deed for a few hundred dollars, plus installation, and have some of these features in the lid itself.

Here's a tip for those who can't wait to take the plunge: You can actually bring one back with you on the plane. It doesn't matter if you don't have time to shop while on your visit to Japan, because you can actually pick one up at the airport gift shop!

I ended up buying a few things, but didn't pick up the toilet seat. I stuck to a model of a samurai warrior, a hat, and a couple of T-shirts as well as some bottles of sake. I'm not sure how many seats they sell in any given day, but I can tell you that I made a few passes by one model in the store and thought about picking it up right then and there. I was already longing for the feel of that warm seat, but then snapped back to reality.

I'm not too good with my hands and figured I would need an electrician and quite possibly a plumber to actually make it work. Otherwise it would end up like most of the things that I buy on a whim—in pieces in some box tucked in the corner of the base-ment or attic. The next time I'd see it would be during a spring cleanup effort or a move to a new house. Knowing my limitations in this regard, and not wanting to spend an additional thousand dollars to have it installed, I kept my toilet seat longing in check. A cold bum would have to do!

The Glories of Automation

I didn't have to install anything as a result of that trip to Japan, but while I was there, I did have to get clued in on the control panel that is used to operate these waste-management wonders. They vary in their complexity, with some of them boasting sophisti-cated remote controls, as I came to learn.

My theory is these remotes could come in handy after you com-pletely destroy your particular bathroom and need to get away quickly. The remote might allow you to flush the toilet without doing any more damage to your nasal passages. It's akin to a remote detonator for the bomb you just dropped. Instead of exploding, it safely deactivates from a comfortable distance.

Besides the heated seat, some with their own thermostats to adjust to your liking, there are plenty of other amazing features. Instead of a bidet sitting next to your toilet like you might see in a fancy hotel, this one has its very own bidet built in to the seat. Push the appropriate button while sitting and a wand appears to shoot a stream of water straight up at your private area. Want your bum cleaned ahead of wiping? Another button produces a different wand that somehow knows how to hit the proper target. It even has a "massage" setting.

Imagine the possibilities. You can enjoy a massage of pulsing warm water, all the while adjusting the beat of the stream. If you like yours steady, no problem. A little more intermittent? You're good. It's like the advertising slogan: "Have it your way!"

Let's say you choose to have the water wand spray your butt. What would you choose next? Most people don't think about this, but the Japanese have. You dry it, but without using your hands. They have a built in dryer that blows warm air on your rear to dry the same spot that just got washed. You've now managed to have your *gluteus maximus* warmed by the seat, your orifice washed by warm water and then dried. What's next? Why not take a swipe and see how everything has worked out? You are looking good!

Now you're ready to make that last move and flush the toilet. Here you have two choices, making this a green solution. You can do the full flush or the half flush. It's your call, as you take the second to final step in your toilet odyssey. *What more could there possibly be?* How about the "power deodorizer" button that creates another blast of warm air that's infused with something to make you as a fresh as a daisy?

Emergency Rear-End Response

As I sat on my private throne at the Capitol Hotel Tokyo, marveling at the engineering that went into my first toilet experience in Japan, I went looking for the flush control. I noticed that there were large buttons on the panel against the wall, but none seemed to indicate flushing. My eyes darted back and forth as I simply couldn't figure out the damn thing. Then it dawned on me that the square button off to the right had to be it.

I didn't have my glasses on and quickly pushed the center of the square. Much to my horror a bright red light came on indicating "EMERGENCY." *Holy shit,* I thought as I went into full panic mode. This thing had to be wired into the main hotel system. I wasn't completely finished yet, and all I could think about was the over-vigilant hotel staff descending on my room in an attempt to rescue me from my predicament. As quickly as I could manage, I headed out of the bathroom looking for the phone. I had checked in only minutes earlier and had just received my bags before I hit the john. Based on how fast the bags arrived after check in I figured they were almost at my door by the time my hand grabbed the handset.

I dialed the operator.

"I'm Okay!" I blurted out when someone answered.

Something came out in Japanese and then quickly switched to English. "Yes, Mr. Murphy. May I help you?"

"I'm good. No emergency here."

That was met with a split second of silence when I quickly added "I don't have an emergency."

I'm guessing she had absolutely no idea what I was referring to in my out-of-breath voice, so I continued on with "I accidentally hit the emergency button in the bathroom and just wanted to let you know that I was fine and not to send anybody."

All of this was being said as I stood there naked, still wondering if some kind of helmeted Japanese maintenance SWAT team was going to burst into my room at any second.

I was trying my hardest not to let the embarrassment of my emergency call button mistake morph into something much worse—having uniformed people charge in to help me as I stood there in my birthday suit. Fortunately, the message was understood and I was spared that nightmare. I noticed that I was suddenly wide awake despite the long trip. The idea of someone barging in on you in this kind of situation will certainly sharpen your senses!

Perfecting the Art of Going

My initial Japanese toilet experience took place in a high-end hotel, but if you think these computerized commodes exist only in these places, you would be wrong. The models and features can vary, but they are literally everywhere.

When you are in someone's home, they are there. Go to a bar or restaurant, and bingo. Riding the bullet train to Kyoto? Got you covered! Or bottomed, as the case may be. I can't recall a single bathroom that I used in my entire stay that didn't have one of these multifunctional high-tech seats of one kind or another. It is simply amazing how pervasive these things are and how some have different features than others. Many of them even lower the lid for you automatically.

Study your instruction manual before using the control panel on this toilet.

Don't be fooled...this thing has a mind of its own.

In a tiny little restaurant in Tokyo, a place with fewer than ten tables, their miniscule bathroom came equipped with one of these amazing things. What made this one remarkable was what happened when you stood in front of it. Like magic the seat slowly raised up on its own and out of the way of any males who are too lazy to raise it with their hand or foot. That was due to the sensor that sits in the back of the seat and discerns what you are about to do. Unbelievable.

The Japanese have perfected the art of the bathroom experience. Nothing else comes close to what they have created. If there were a contest to determine who had the cleanest bums in the world, all would have to agree that Japan stands apart. Or put another way, they surely do sit apart, at least in the bathroom.

24

Japan: After the Tsunami

My travels to Japan and the high-tech bathroom experience came exactly three months after the devastating earthquake and tsunami that struck the coast. I was there to spend seven nights on the ground between Sendai and Tokyo, filming updates from a tourism perspective.

Sendai was the town you heard so much about on television. It suffered the full force of the tsunami that dragged boats, cars and houses miles from where they once stood or floated. The images you saw on television were dramatic to say the least.

We were all glued to our television sets, watching the earth get swallowed by a rolling wave that didn't seem to ever want to stop. We watched intently as houses and entire neighborhoods that stood there just moments earlier suddenly no longer existed. We thought about the people who were lost and became numb. This went on for weeks as the twenty-four-hour news cycle continued.

Even though the networks covered this horrific event extensively, it was hard to really appreciate its full impact until you drove down a main road miles from the sea and passed a large boat on the side of the road. That's what I did, and it was disturbing to actually see something like that in person. The shocking, severe dislocation of boats, cars, homes and lives was surreal in the extreme.

The Japanese people rallied and set about the task of rebuilding their lives without any drama. There was no looting or sordid behavior like you see following so many other disasters. These people simply acted with the resolve to move on and make things right. There wasn't much additional drama to report as the story moved off the front pages, and it quickly was replaced by the Anthony Weiner sex scandal and what has become known as "Weinergate." We went from one extreme to the other; from a historic and profound life-changing natural event to a sordid diversion as pathetic as Weiner's wiener. That's journalism in the new millennium, I guess.

Shelter and Survival

Being in Japan so soon after the tsunami, I learned from the local residents what it was like to live through a disaster of that magnitude. When the earthquake struck it took over three minutes for the earth to stop shaking. While that was happening 1,600 people at the Sendai International Airport were running for open ground, fearful of a building collapse.

With power out, the tsunami warnings couldn't be heard, but one airport executive we spoke with told us about it being picked up on someone's cell phone. Alerted to the news of the pending wave, hundreds of people immediately rushed back in through the airport doors and headed up the steps, just moments after they had been evacuated. They headed for the second and third floors, which they believed would offer relative safety. That strategy turned out to be a lifesaver, as forty minutes after the initial quake a ten-foot wall of water came blasting through the terminal and airport property, sweeping away cars, planes and anything else in its path.

Those who were huddled on the terminal's top floors described the inundation as a roar that was married with the sound of breaking glass as windows and doors shattered in the water's path. You can see what it was like from the video we shot of the reconstruction, where I show you the direction of the water and some scenes from that day.

Sadly, the impact of the quake and tsunami continues to this day, even as planes are taking off and landing at the repaired airport. Some travelers are afraid to come to Japan due to the radiation leaks at the Fukushima Daiichi nuclear power-generating facility.

Visiting Sendai, Japan after the tsunami in 2011.

They forget that the site of the reactor is nowhere near many of the tourist areas that are popular with travelers.

That's one of the major reasons we ventured to Japan, to see things firsthand. In addition to our Travel Unscripted approach, we are sometimes called upon to set the record straight after the major news outlets move on to the latest breaking news. In that way we help travel agents, suppliers and their customers see the reality of travel in a particular area or region. In this case, it's not about showcasing the experience; it's simply about reassuring them that things are quite normal and can be explored safely.

Japan gets more than two percent of its gross domestic product from travel and tourism. The impact of tourism and the disaster went well beyond this number. Other Asian nations, Hawaii, and the mainland United States also felt the loss of those travelers on their end. We couldn't help in regards to the outbound situation from Japan, but thought we could bring people a perspective from what was going on from an inbound standpoint.

It isn't exactly dramatic to show a city named Sendai with a million people as its people simply go about their day-to-day lives. The same can be said for the far larger city of Tokyo. Warnings still hang in the air as this book nears publication, not unlike the radiation that has leaked from the nuclear plant. Travelers need to distinguish between broad, general warnings, and the reality of what's really happening on the ground.

With little drama we put a spotlight on Japan and focused on what they really need…simply more tourists.

25

Lost in Translation

Fate is a bitch. Even if I had taken the time to hire a team of battle-hardened tarot-card readers, Hindu mystics and astrologic star scanners, I could never have imagined that my life would intersect so improbably with that of Anderson Cooper.

Well, it didn't exactly intersect with the popular white-haired anchorman, but something strange did happen. The whole off-the-wall state of affairs kicked in on our first real location trip as a production team on a visit to China in 2006. At that time, Cooper was already hosting *AC360* for CNN and had emerged as a news personality with a global face recognition factor verging on 99.9 percent. The 0.1 percent would include a few stray Tibetan sheepherders and random others.

Well, my big break in the travel business was going to be China! We were traveling with a company that had recently intro-duced what they term their "VIP tour" of the Middle Kingdom. The company had been known as a major Hawaii wholesaler for years, but through acquisitions had expanded into the Asia market. They wanted to showcase this new tour by having us, along with other journalists, get a first-hand and in-depth experience into what makes China unique.

I definitely was down with that. However, I didn't really give much thought to one of the most important factors you must consider when you cross over into strange and unfamiliar places: *making yourself understood.*

Like most of my countrymen, I suffer from the standard American Arrogance, usually stated like this: "Oh, they speak English everywhere, especially in the higher-end hotels." Well, yes they do, it turns out. Sort of. Various grunts and hand gestures can be figured out down to their root meaning. But step outside a hotel and all bets are off when it comes to understanding virtually anything. It's basically "point and move!" This clear cluelessness to the language, along with the always-dependable cultural misunderstandings and disconnects, are where the fun starts.

The difference between expectation and reality turned out to be a very large canyon on this little jaunt. There have been times in my life where I was dumber than a ball-field hotdog and this was one of them. Throughout this entire trip our experiences had a definite *Lost in Translation* quality. Well, at least they allowed me to come up with several useful rules that could save you the same uncomfortable scenarios.

Rule #1: If you can talk a good game, you can usually worm your way out of an ominous situation...but not always

The better your persuasive communications skills, generally the better off you'll be. Failing to talk or otherwise skillfully maneuver yourself out of a dicey situation usually leaves you 1) on your ass, 2) with your wallet significantly lighter or 3) in a very uncom-fortable circumstance...maybe for as long as twenty hours.

DATELINE: THE PLANE. Asia travel is an ordeal you prepare for. If you have been harboring a secret desire to read through, say, Tolstoy's *War and Peace* or Proust's *Le Recherche du Temps Perdu*, this is the time to pack them up for the long haul—hopefully on your Kindle or iPad, because their print editions are so humongous that they become weaponized if accidently pushed off a plastic tray table onto your foot. Any way you cut it, it's a long flight.

In this case, the first part of this trip was shaping up to be unusually rough because we were flying from the U.S. east coast through San Francisco to get to our final destination in Beijing. In case you didn't know it, a stop in San Francisco adds about six hours to your travel time versus a nonstop flight. Taking this unfortunate route from the east coast means you're looking at something approaching twenty hours!

Ever the strategist, I quickly engineered some good luck, found an old first-class upgrade certificate, and managed to talk my way into the forward cabin for the twelve-hour leg from San Francisco to Beijing. Unfortunately, my traveling partner Nick Choo wasn't so fortunate, or at least didn't think as fast. Not only did he get stuck in steerage for the entire journey, he ended up jammed in a window seat next to the head of public relations for the tour company that was bringing us on the trip!

At one point after takeoff I walked to the back of the plane to seek out Nick and his seat companion, the PR guy. What I witnessed there was kind of pathetic. Nick weighed about 130 pounds back then, while the PR guy was at least 240 by my estimate. They looked like Big Bird and Oscar, or maybe little Mike Bloomberg and Chris Christie on some kind of crazy political family vacation. And, of course, we know how much some PR folks like to talk.

I figured that the best Nick could hope for was that he had stocked up on some serious sleep medication that would knock him out somewhere over the Pacific, and fast!

Throughout the outbound flight Nick squirmed in his seat and tried to avoid small talk. He is known as No Talk Nick for a reason, as talking to him is like pulling teeth. As Nick tells it, he attempted to alternately feign sleep and exhaustion, both anathema to the PR mentality. The poor tour company guy would be talking to a blank wall for that entire flight…and essentially that's what he did. I didn't know who I pitied the most, him or Nick.

Rule #2: If you think you understand what you're getting, you are wrong

Cultural differences can mess with the best-laid plans and the most exciting expectations.

DATELINE: MASSAGE. We ultimately extricated ourselves from the airport on the other end, and our tour began with a few nights at the Shangri La Hotel in Beijing. The first thing I did after taking a shower was wander around. We had arrived later in the day, and after we got something to eat we had nothing to do until early morning.

After that interminable flight I figured I could really use a massage, so I headed to the elevator bank and headed to the hotel spa that was still open at 11:00 p.m. I wasn't sure what to expect when I arrived, but was more than pleasantly surprised when a beautiful woman greeted me and happily escorted me to the room where I would be getting my treatment. So far so good, I thought! My body tingled as I anticipated the next step in the process.

I was thinking it was my lucky day to have such a beautiful masseuse until I heard a loud bark in Mandarin followed by what must have been commands to leave the room. The lithe beauty who had just brought me to the room visibly cowered while she crept away. I wasn't sure what that was all about and didn't really care. I was ready for my well-deserved and sure-to-be-rewarding massage after more than twenty-four hours of travel. Hey...I'd earned it.

I laid down on the table and covered my exposed rear with the towel that was provided. With my face in the hole of the table I expectantly waited for the knock that was soon to come. It did, and I lifted my head to greet my masseuse again.

What entered the room was technically female, but more of the... um...muscular variety. On first glance, my instinct was that this woman had been saucing up on what bodybuilders call "juice" or anabolic steroids, as she looked a bit like a professional wrestler. She even looked like a guy who actually worked for us, named Mole—or at least his female alter ego.

When you are expecting the nice petite woman to return to give you your massage and the female version of Mole shows up, it's not a good day. Mole is a big guy, and if you are a woman you don't want to be compared to him, as he is about 220 pounds of solid muscle.

I suddenly knew that I was about to experience a world of hurt on that table as she grunted and got to work. As I laid there I couldn't get Mole's face out of my head, making for the worst massage I've ever experienced. There were times during this

My man Mole. Massage, anyone?

unfortunate session where I felt like I was being run over by a small pickup truck. The sense of this violation was more than I could bear, and the massage couldn't end soon enough.

It's funny how my airline exhaustion—even in first class—translated into this Twilight Zone episode that was supposed to be a relaxing massage. All of my preconceived ideas, even fantasies, were right on the front lines when I met the lovely Chinese hostess at the massage place. But somewhere along the line, what I expected, and what I saw got sliced, diced, flipped and turned and translated into a roller derby slammer who could have sent me to the hospital. Getting lost in translation can leave you in many unexpected places.

But wait, it gets even better.

Rule #3: You are who they think you are

Whatever they say you are, they're right.

DATELINE: THE WHITE EMPEROR. The time had come to get down to business. Given the history we were standing on, and the tour company's introduction of a new product in China for VIP guests, we decided to use the dramatic setting of the Great Wall as the backdrop for an interview with the president of their company at the time, who I'll call Roger.

In the crude calculus of media, I have to admit, the Great Wall is a cliché. Everybody on the planet has seen a picture of the thing at least once. The fact that it's pretty much a pointless exercise in human ego and frailty and failed to keep the invaders out of China is beside the point. It exudes power. On a TV screen it's massive and overwhelming and just reeks "power narrative." TV executives love that stuff. Eat it up with a spoon.

Historically, the Great Wall is a monument to the power of the Chinese emperors who commanded masses of human beings to build it, stone by stone. In stretches as short as a few years, an army of people being directed by various emperors constructed major sections of this wall. There certainly was no mechanized equipment back in the fifth century B.C. and still nothing along those lines in the sixteenth century when construction finally stopped.

So the team and I did our "professional interview configuration on the Great Wall," with a single camera and natural lighting correctly positioned on Roger for optimal effect on video. I was dressed for my best on-camera foreign correspondent act, all crisp with blazer and trimmings. I got into the interview and asked Roger a variety of questions about their new product and what it might mean for travel agents and their customers. With our hookup, travel agents all over the United States would be able to see our report just a few hours later via online video.

I was so busy with all the setup and interview preparations that I had not noticed the level of interest that our modest interview setup was generating among the many people visiting the site. The Great Wall itself is such a staggeringly overwhelming experience that it never occurred to me for a nanosecond that a few guys with TV cameras would attract a moment's attention. I proved to be stunningly incorrect. After the first segment of the interview completed I turned momentarily to look back and there were a handful of Chinese tourists snapping photos as if we were actually celebrities.

I shot a "WTF?" look at Nick, who came over and whispered in my ear. "It appears that they think you are some kind of American reporter."

"Let's tell 'em I'm Anderson Cooper!" I told Nick, laughing. Then again, how is that going to work out? I still have brown hair, to say nothing of the fact that I look nothing at all like Anderson Cooper physically! As I looked around I smiled as a few more people with cameras snapped away—*snap snap snap snap snap*—so I waved back. What the hell else was there to do?

This only encouraged them more. More people stopped by and next thing you know I'm posing with God knows whom on the Great Wall as they continue to mistake me for someone else.

At this point some of the international tourists began picking up the scent that Somebody Important might be on the hangout here. The Americans and Euros were, of course, less likely to confuse me with CNN's boyish news guy, so that hypothesis quickly hit the dumpster with them. There were a handful of random guesses from the back corners of the peanut gallery "He's that watzizname from See BS, Sixty min ya' know" and "I think he does the CNBC financial something or other"—all amidst a vast clattering clickstream of camera shots.

It all goes to show that if we don't know something, we tend to make it up. Getting lost in translation is half the time about how people make unwarranted assumptions and then just run with them. The Chinese were apparently ready to confer upon me the crown of global White News Emperor. Now *that* would have been interesting. Could I have ordered them to build a New Great Wall?

Rule #4: Different audiences hear different things

We all hear what we want to hear, don't we?

DATELINE: THE GENTLEMAN INTERPRETER. I now come to one of the more perilous and bizarre tales of our tour. Of course, anything involving interpreters is always edgy and laced with risk. After my experience in China and a few other international bumpy rides, I would have to say candidly that I am ready to stack up "interpretation" and "translation" right up there in the Dark Arts categories along with various forms of sorcery, incantation, casting of spells, and turning frogs into princes. I will discuss this point in more detail later, but for now I will continue the narrative. You will see what I mean, very clearly.

The trip organizer had scheduled a number of meetings and dinners to introduce their VIP guests to one executive director after another. I lost track, but each time we ended up in a new place or at a special museum or attraction we had a lovely greeting. We were introduced to what we were told was a regional or museum director, but wouldn't have a clue as no English was actually spoken by these individuals. That didn't stop us from having some afternoon or morning tea and learning more about a particular area or site.

One of the people leading the trip was a gentleman who had deep ties to the Chinese mainland, named Cheng. His connections made a "behind the scenes" tour a reality for a select few of us as we were introduced to some incredible sites. If you aren't connected in China you won't be getting much accomplished. Indeed, without connections you are on your own. This guy had them in spades.

At each meeting Cheng would make the introductions and let us know who the individual we were meeting with was. He would speak in Mandarin to our host and then turn to us and give us the background. More conversations would go on followed by his translation.

A funny thing happened on the way to that translation. As we all sat there and heard the English version from Cheng, our host/ interpreter, we thought we were hearing the exact translation. That wasn't exactly the case.

Fortunately I had my right hand guy, Nick Choo. He was raised in Taiwan and Malaysia, and is fluent in English as well as Mandarin. When these conversations started he would lean in and tell me what was actually being said, not what we were hearing.

Here I am sitting in this room with what I will call Interpreter Number 1: Cheng. He is telling the tour organizer and the rest of us a line of unmitigated pond sewage to the effect that "I created this absolutely wonderful travel experience for you, and the executive director has personally thanked me for making it possible for such a wonderful group to be here in his museum."

That is when he is speaking English. When he is speaking Chinese, he is spouting a line of equally toxic chemical effluent to the effect that "Through my international contacts, I brought these top American journalists to you so that they will tell all of their readers in America why they should come to your museum."

Now let me turn to Interpreter Number 2, Nick! He didn't trust Cheng from the get go—I think it maybe was the sense Nick had that Cheng was a Chinese version of P. T. Barnum. So Nick kept a running commentary as he translated the Mandarin commentaries of our erstwhile interpreter. It went something like this:

In English (for our benefit)	In Chinese (for our Chinese hosts' benefit)
What Cheng told us the MUSEUM DIRECTOR was saying	What Cheng told the museum director WE were saying
The executive director has personally thanked me for bringing all of you here to learn about his wonderful museum.	The executive of the U.S. company has personally thanked me for my wisdom in selecting your wonderful museum.
Thank you for being here and for making such a long journey to learn about our museum.	Thank you and Mr. Cheng for your hospitality and it is our honor to enjoy the greatness of your museum.
I hope you will be able to spend some time here and enjoy the museum and its wonderful collections. We are very proud of them.	We thank Mr. Cheng for bringing us to one of the best world-class museums we have ever seen in our lives!
He said that I am welcome to bring any of you back in the future where I will host a special reception for all of you after the museum closes. They will serve you dinner and bring in special entertainment.	Thanks to Mr. Cheng's intimate contacts, we will come back again in the near future to enjoy your museum again with more people and you can serve them at a greater level.

So while everyone else was bobbing their heads in agreement and giving kudos to Cheng, we were laughing and enjoying the misdirection. He made himself the center of the universe! It certainly worked to impress the entire staff from the company as well as all of the guests and journalists.

At the conclusion of the evening, I asked Nick to have a conversation with Cheng in his native tongue. I wanted him to know that we were on to his game and very much aware of the actual translation. Cheng's eyes got big as saucers as Nick spoke and both of us smiled. Checkmate my friend, checkmate.

In this case we were not so much lost in translation as hijacked by an interpreter, but it's kind of the same thing. The difference between what things really mean and what we think they mean is where the telling points of life are. But stay tuned...it gets even more interesting.

Rule #5: Your expectations may be dangerous

What we expect is based on what we know from the past, not what is coming from the future.

DATELINE: WARRIOR DANCES. I now turn to the most lurid and insanely bizarre tale of my initial trip to China. It is only fitting that it is a tale centered upon warriors and various images and impressions and expectations that we have when traveling to such a faraway place as China. The travel website "reality" of pictures and images creates a sense of the place as a kind of amusement park. Once you arrive, of course, you must deal with the brutal reality of muscle-bound female masseurs and circus-hustler interpreters. But it gets better, trust me.

Xian is the site of the famed armies of terracotta warriors, discovered by farmers in 1974. They were created to accompany an ancient Chinese emperor as part of his tomb complex, and have become one of the principal stations on the tourist itinerary. We had plans to see the warriors on the day after we arrived in the ancient capital, but at the Sheraton Hotel that night we were looking for something to do.

Nick had made friends with a front desk clerk, who was from Penang, where he had attended school. The clerk suggested a happening bar in the old part of the city, about fifteen minutes away from us.

So, we set off immediately to check this place out. Luckily I had Nick who would be my Mandarin translator for this trip, as there was no way I could have gone to a native Chinese club like this without him to guide me and do the ordering.

When we arrived we immediately noticed that the establishment was a large rectangular shape with a DJ booth at one end and a dance floor extending out in the opposite direction. Just above and behind the DJ booth you could see two very hot girls dancing on some kind of platform. The decision was made: We were sitting under the platform, as close as we could possibly get!

As we leaned back with our warm beers we still couldn't believe our good luck. The two nubile young women were gyrating and going wild to the pulsating beat. One was dressed in a short plaid skirt, the other in a pair of tight-fitting hot pants. It was an impressive sight even for us world-weary travelers, and a welcome change from all the dinners and speeches.

So far so good. Booming music, drinks, the usual lighting stunts, some very stunning looking young women (100 points) dancing wildly (1,000 points), even suggestively (5,000 points), in hot pants (off the charts). So everything here was totally, seriously and insanely within my comfort zone, which is to say that it lined up with my expectations.

I was reveling in our great fortune when the scene on the platform changed suddenly...and disturbingly. The song came to an end and the hot dancing girl slithered off the platform. A new hard-hitting tune started up, but this time two dudes jumped up on the platforms and continued the dancing. One guy was wearing some kind of rubber skin suit that stretched over his body, complete with hot pants. The other one was wearing suspenders and short shorts with high boots. So now we're sitting here—very, *very* close—and looking up at Xian warriors of a sort, gyrating half-naked all over the dance floor.

I glanced over at Nick. He seemed frozen, his suddenly sweaty, red face gazing up into the pulsating lights, his mouth slightly agape, with a sort of chilling animalistic-looking fear in his eyes— kind of like a doomed opossum caught in headlights on a deep-woods road someplace in Alabama. He didn't move, and I wasn't even sure that he was breathing.

At this juncture my survival mechanism kicked in. I told myself that there would be more women coming up shortly, and that we could wait this out. These guys would...um, quickly do their thing ...and everything would be right with the world again.

That didn't quite happen. Off to my immediate right I noticed two guys and a girl dancing together like many friends some-times do. Then the woman disengaged and the two guys really started to get down with one another. As we watched trans-fixed, they ran their hands all over each other, and one guy pulled off the other's shirt. They made their way around and behind the bar without missing a beat while they caressed each other's skin.

I didn't dare look at Nick.

This continued on for another minute, making us believe that they actually worked here and this was part of the "show." That assumption ended quickly when the guy working behind the bar yelled at them to get out of there and put their shirts on.

At that moment I turned to Nick and said, "Hey man, what the hell kind of place is this?" He seemed to have regained some equilib-rium and shrugged. This whole scene seemed radically out of step with reality, given its setting in the ancient city of Xian, and in a country that's not particularly known for self-expression!

In retrospect I guess I really shouldn't have been so shocked. So much about China is about appearances that have other realities hidden behind them.

Lessons Learned

Throughout this trip to China, I continually found that expectations I had or things I sought to do were often lost in translation and became twisted into something else entirely. Whether it was the female muscle masseur, the Chinese crowd confusing me with some unnamed media guy, the Chinese P. T. Barnum, Cheng, talking out of both sides of his mouth or the Xian Warriors enthusiastically pawing each other in a dance club, I just continually found myself blindsided, slack-jawed and occasionally pie-eyed with surprise at how things played out around me.

The bottom line is that I learned to roll with the punches and take hurdles gracefully. Now, after a few years of this stuff, I can tell you that nothing surprises me.

Nothing at all.

Alarming Situation	What They Say	What They Really Mean	Potential for Catastrophe
At the Airport			
You are number 200 in line to check your bags at Heathrow.	"The line is moving along."	"Dream on, sucker."	Not only will you miss your initial flight, and your connecting flights, the airline will find a way to route you to Beijing via somewhere in Malaysia.
You are hoping for an upgrade so you won't have to sit in a middle seat between two *Biggest Loser* contestants.	"We have open seats. Only a few first class haven't checked in yet."	"You bozo. You're going to be stuck in steerage and it's a five hour flight, so get used to it."	You beg the Redcoat to reroute you on a different flight even if it does mean another leg through Guam.

Alarming Situation	What They Say	What They Really Mean	Potential for Catastrophe
At the Airport (continued)			
You observe that there is no aircraft parked at your gate and it is ten minutes from your listed departure time.	"We have a slight delay due to weather irregularities."	"Your 777 is grounded at its last destination thanks to Hurricane Pepito, honey, so get ready to sleep on the couch."	You amuse yourself by connecting with the Aggrieved Customer website, spending the entire evening doing a drop kick on every aspect of this airline's customer service, complete with rich and barely printable metaphors.
Sightseeing			
Touring the ancient pagoda of the Monkey Lord, you ask innocently about the dungeon tower across the pond.	"The great lord built this beautiful pagoda and gardens as an expression of his deep spirituality."	"The great lord was a sadistic pervo and I'm not going to go into all that dungeon stuff because I got a whole bunch of blue-haired ladies from Kansas City on this damn tour who couldn't handle it, okay chump?"	Belligerent guide suggests *sotto voce* that he will sequester you in the torture chamber during the Extreme Dim Sum tour lunch buffet if you don't shut your trap, pronto.
Standing outside the ancient forbidden mystic temple devoted to a human-animal combo god creature entity.	"The ancients contemplated the God's presence in absolute silence for the sacred temple was designed to echo even the tiniest sound for hours."	"I know you are a bunch of meatheaded tourists, but even you can get this. SHUT UP when we go inside this thing—it will blow your brains out with boom-echoes if anybody starts talking too loud."	Squirming with bio-urgency, you follow the others into the temple and ask your traveling companion, "Did you see anywhere I can TAKE A PISS?" The expression "TAKE A PISS" echo-explodes from the God's mouth for an eternity.

26

Moscow: Contrasts and Contradictions

Let me warn you: If you're traveling to Moscow, under no circumstances should you ignore this advice. Don't make exceptions due to peer pressure or because you were caught up in the moment.

Whatever you do, never try to match a Muscovite drink for drink. It will cause you nothing but pain and embarrassment.

Moscow folk, and perhaps Russians in general, seem to possess genetic engineering different from the rest of us. Their livers seem to be constructed of some sort of otherworldly titanium alloy—the Cray super-computer of livers—metabolizing alcohol at the speed of out-like-a-light.

A single Russian can consume inordinate amounts of liquor, with "inordinate" being defined as enough cheap hooch to put the entirety of Sweden under the table. Your average Russian considers the phrase "last call" to be both a joke and an insult. Even after hours spent slamming the contents of a shot-glass pyramid, your average Muscovite functions as if he's imbibed in nothing stronger than a sip of Diet Coke.

Don't get me wrong: This is not some kind of arbitrary ethnic stereotype It's a personal observation that resulted from five nights spent drinking and partying with a diverse group of people that call Moscow their home. Lots of cultures brag on their drinking prowess, but they're all amateurs in comparison to the residents of the country that gave us Sputnik, the Cold War, a wacky collection of inbred Tsars and Tsarinas, full-tilt communism and Maria Sharapova. Russians are the real deal. They walk the walk and talk the talk.

In short, they put their vodka where their mouth is...constantly.

Every member of my group could drink. The forty-something attorney and twenty-something fashion designer were both grand masters in guzzling. The former weighed about 180 pounds and was in good shape. The latter weighed about fifteen pounds soaking wet. Size and shape doesn't matter. If these two had gone toe-to-toe in a regulation, fifteen-round booze-bout, the odds would have been dead even.

Let me put it this way. I didn't have to wear a watch the entire time I was in Moscow. It quickly became apparent that my new-found friends ordered another tumbler of high-octane potato juice every ten minutes.

My second warning about traveling to Moscow. Again, disregard this lesson at your own risk...or at least at your own risk of catching the sort of bug that leads to painful urination:

Women in Moscow bars will stare at you. Do not stare back, no matter how gorgeous they happen to be. More important... NEVER SMILE!

I was given this warning by a friend who has done business in Russia for well over a decade. I don't doubt his knowledge, but I wanted to know why.

"What do you mean," I asked him. "Why shouldn't I smile?"

"Women in Russian bars tend to be extremely beautiful and extremely forward. They'll stare at you, and if you stare back you're going to be approached."

"And that's a bad thing?" I said with a smirk.

"It's hard to tell the civilians from the pros," he explained.

I later learned that he was right. The women do stare, or at least they stare after knocking back a few dozen fifths of vodka; it's just part of the culture. But the pros...they'll stare with a look that is far more predatory, like you're the mouse and they're the cat. If you've had a few drinks yourself, it's hard to tell the difference.

Drinking and Staring

My first real taste of Moscow's two most popular contact sports—drinking and staring—occurred during my second night in the city. My business friend introduced me to the owner of one of the city's law firms. Alexie was gracious in his offer to take my crew and me to local hotspots not on the typical tourist itinerary. It sounded perfect—I wanted the true flavor of Moscow, to view it through the eyes of a native.

We started at Bar Luch, a trendy joint featuring food, drinks, dancing and a bar more than a hundred feet long. We grabbed some seats and immediately noticed two attractive girls sitting at a table near ours. Alexie was disappointed in the turnout that evening, and apologized profusely for the lack of eye-candy, although I can't remember asking for any! He was even more disappointed when the girls paid their bill and left. To give credit where it's due, he did attempt to make small talk with them as they were on their way out. They showed zero interest in any of us.

Alexie seemed to be resigned to a slow evening that could cause him to slip into one of those morose, dark moods for which Russians are legendary. I tried to get my production crew a little more energized, because they weren't exactly an engaging pair at that or any time, but no such luck. It fell on me to keep the conversation going with Alexie and figure out what the nightlife scene in Moscow could present to us. It seemed to me that he just needed to catch his second wind. Like a laser-focused hockey forward, he hadn't scored yet, but had merely taken his first shot on goal. He knew his city, and there would be plenty more opportunities.

Alexie rationalized that we were visiting during what was the peak vacation season for Muscovites. As a result, the nightlife was much slower than normal, he said. In fact, he insisted that we join him on the following evening, a Friday. He said he had a hockey game that night, but he and friends would be out around midnight and we'd be welcome to join them. He added that he'd be hitting his usual haunts. That sounded interesting, as I was eager to meet more locals and get a feel for the "real" Moscow.

We spent the next hour or so drinking vodka like it was water, and I was at my limit. That's the good thing about me these days. I definitely know my personal point of no return and I was at it with a full day of filming ahead. I politely declined the last round and suggested that we head back to the hotel, saving our energies for the following day and evening.

And that's when Alexie told me that he wanted to make one final stop that night at what he described as a traditional Moscow bar. It was a place where—his words, not mine—the girls would be a bit on the "easy" side. *What the hell,* I thought. *Let's try it.*

Turbulent Flying in Hookerland

The Russians have a talent for understatement. Easy? Alexie led us straight to an establishment called Night Flight, but it could just have easily been called "Hookers R Us." Every woman in the place was a pro. The staring and stalking took on an entirely new meaning; the gals were hungry for business and they weren't wasting any time.

It was a relatively quiet night in the place and the women out-numbered the men by about five to one. As we stood at the bar and used our entry coupon for our one included drink I felt a hand on my upper back. Not the friendly pat of a buddy slap, but instead a sensual touch that came from a young woman. As I turned my head she lightly ran her hand up and down my spine and smiled. She launched into a well-rehearsed spiel that was as mechanical as a flight attendant's safety instructions. Her ambition was obvious, but her delivery needed work. She did punctuate her patter with creative and highly exaggerated hand motions, and by the time she finished it was clear that she wanted to put my tray table in the upright position. I also knew that I was not supposed to get up, or move, until the seatbelt light was off.

I'm certain she felt that we were taxiing down the runway, about to achieve takeoff. Dollar signs were in her eyes—I had listened for too long—and her presentation moved more into telemar-keter mode. She vividly shared the many ideas she had to make me happy, a little like a DirecTV operator describing the untold joy I would receive if I'd simply fork over my credit-card number and purchase a ten-year subscription to Cinemax.

I can't say she was rude or even mildly irritated when I politely declined. She simply turned, walked away and sought out a more willing buyer.

I began looking for my crew. Nick and Gene were doing their best to fend off the approaches of their own working girls on the prowl. They were both employing the "Me no understand Engrish" strategy. When that failed, they resorted to the "I have no money" excuse. The girls weren't buying it. Russian prostitutes are tenacious as bulldogs, and Gene's gal decided to help him find his wallet. She was patting him down like a disgruntled TSA agent with a fondness for strip searches; he was trying to fend her off without being impolite. She was nearing the end of the runway, but wasn't concerned about any sort of crash.

I tapped her on the shoulder in an attempt to give Gene some relief.

"He has no money," I told her with a smile. "He's broke, tapped out, too poor to pay attention. He lives with his mother...in the basement."

She turned her head, scanned me like the hooker version of an MRI machine, and replied, "Go away, I don't like old men!"

Old man? Jesus. I know I'm not exactly young, but I never counted on a hooker being the first woman to ever call me an old man. That was so disturbing I almost ordered another drink.

I was picking up Moscow culture—or at least the underside of Moscow culture—by osmosis. What is typical in some societies is utterly foreign in others. It had become blatantly apparent that this bar, Night Flight, was where local business guys brought foreign clients to (literally) consummate a deal.

One guy, an American who I had recognized from my flight from London two days earlier, strolled into the bar just as I was having that exact thought. A swarm of Russian hookers turned as one and bee lined in his direction. It was as if Johnny Depp had just walked through the doors of the Viper Club in LA. I don't know if the unsuspecting American was pleased, confused or scared.

I didn't want to seem unappreciative of Alexie's hospitality, but this wasn't my idea of a good time. I made the most of it by asking some questions of the women who continued to approach me. It was a fun exercise, with my standard line being that I was an American journalist researching economic opportunities for Russian women. They asked in graphic detail what I might want; I asked them about their investment strategies and oil production in Siberia. Word spread quickly—asking a hooker about the International Monetary Fund can be amusing—and I was soon left to my own devices.

But, not all of them were dissuaded. Despite her earlier aborted landing, the woman who had first approached me reappeared. She again ran her hand up and down my back, asking me how I liked it. I told her she had a great touch, but I still wasn't interested in taking her or anyone else back to my hotel room. I did make a counter-offer on the freestanding back tickle.

"How about $20 if you stand there for ten minutes doing that?" I asked.

With a shake of her head and a look of disgust she turned and walked away.

Alexie was surprised and sad when I told him that the crew and I needed to get going. We had only been in Night Flight for half an hour, and that was about twenty-eight minutes too many. I could see he was feeling insulted so I quickly added that this wasn't exactly what we were looking for. I brought up venereal disease, thinking that was a logic to which any guy could relate.

"Who wants to bring home an STD anyway?" I asked.

"You don't have to worry about that," he replied. "These girls are very expensive."

Once more, cultures vary. In Alexie's world money buys disease-free happiness. Somebody should call up syphilis and herpes and explain that they are henceforth forbidden to infect high-dollar prostitutes, for I don't think they got the memo.

Alexie looked at me like I was an idiot. I was about to learn that my mistake in understanding this world would lead to what I call "one and done" in the local host department.

Alexie's demeanor seemed to change immediately. He became a bit patronizing and bored, as if he was trying to explain calculus to a stray cat. I knew we were only a short distance to our hotel and suggested he stay and we head out, but he insisted on dropping us off on his way to his home. We conferred about the next evening and made our plans to meet up. Hopefully it wouldn't involve hookers or a drip IV of Stolichnaya.

He must have been less than thrilled or impressed with me and the crew as I never saw or heard from Alexie again. He dropped us off at the hotel and disappeared from our lives. An email the next day went unanswered and we decided to find some different ways to get that experience. I'd have to gather the inside scoop on the Moscow scene via another method. With any luck, I thought, we'd learn everything we needed to know from the new guide we were hiring.

That just goes to show what you get for thinking.

Tatiana

"We have secured a young guide to take you around the city and give you a different perspective."

That's how our planning representative phrased it when she called to say she had hired an escort that fit perfectly with our plans. This was different. During most of our travels we're matched

Never get into a drinking contest with a Moscovite.

with an "experienced" guide, meaning *older.* The bureaucrats of any given region's travel division usually want to lead with their best; they typically give us the people who have been doing their job the longest.

More times than not we end up with a knowledgeable guide who, though maybe a bit boring, can recite facts, figures and historical minutiae with machine-gun efficiency. The downside of these older guides is that we sometimes get pigeonholed into visiting the same locations frequented by every other tourist. That's a hindrance when you're seeking the novel and unique.

I was both happy and relieved to learn our guide would be "young." But, once more, we were in Moscow; you have to keep in mind that this is a place where none of the normal rules apply. The male life expectancy in Russia is fifty-seven; the average woman lives about ten years longer. I was guessing that "young" might be defined as someone in their twenties. I hoped that, at the very least, she would be old enough to drive.

I need not have worried.

I'd spoken on the phone with Tatiana, our new guide, on the previous night. She said she'd meet me in the hotel lobby the next morning. I told her it was a small hotel, and that we'd find each other without a problem. I started to ask what she looked like, but the call ended before I had a chance. I wasn't concerned about connecting. I'd just look for the young guide with the credentials hanging around her neck.

The next morning I wandered around the small lobby, wondering why my guide was late. I stepped outside, saw my crew waiting with our driver, and scanned the street. Nobody knew where she was. I returned to the lobby and noticed an older woman with an

ID necklace. She certainly was a guide, but was far too old to be ours. She looked about seventy.

Wrong again. So much for that younger perspective we'd hoped to experience. This was our guide, and I swore for the 1,000th time never to believe a bureaucrat. Tatiana was clearly in the twilight of her career. In fact, she was in the twilight of her second career; before becoming a guide she had retired from her job as a college professor. I don't know what she did prior to that, but I suspect that Peter the Great carried her high-school graduation picture.

We learned plenty from Tatiana over the next few days, most of it unsolicited. She was a wealth of knowledge, which was to be expected from someone who was in her teen years when dirt was born. She informed us early on that she was a committed socialist who longed for the days before perestroika. She felt that things were far better in Russia before Gorbachev screwed it all up. I guess it's easy to get nostalgic for the good old days of gulags, mass starvation, and the KGB.

It's always interesting to view people and events through a different set of eyes. Travel, and Tatiana, provided me that opportunity in Russia. She had lived through two different economic realities (and three or four geologic eras) so who am I to argue with what was better for her? People should be allowed to choose how they want to live, so long as they attempt to respect that others might prefer a different option.

People make choices all the time and sometimes these choices result in some negative situations. Tatiana, however, was a bit dogmatic in her opinions.

Take food. Tatiana thought that the government should mandate that only chemical-free, organic foods could be grown, sold, or consumed. People should eat healthily, like when she was a girl and the tribe would go out and kill a wooly mammoth. Her dietary theories were somewhat in contrast to some of her personal habits, as she educated us on proper living while chain-smoking one cigarette after another.

"What about all the chemicals in cigarettes?" I asked. That got me a shrug and a dirty look. Tatiana was not big on logic.

By my estimate our guide smoked between three and four packs a day. We wouldn't let her smoke in our van, but every time we pulled over to shoot some footage she leapt from the vehicle and fired up another few cancer sticks. She was like a small child on a long car trip, constantly asking us how long we would be at the next stop. It wasn't about time; it wasn't about bathroom breaks. It was all about how many smokes she could inhale within a short window of opportunity. At one stop her cigarette break consisted of eight cigarettes. Now that's some world-class smoking.

Spending time with a person who differed so greatly from me, and in so many ways, was interesting indeed. I'm a capitalist; she was a socialist. She smoked like a chimney with bronchitis, and I'm an ardent anti-tobacco sort of guy. Still, Tatiana was so odd that it was hard not to like her.

One of our funniest conversations occurred when she saw me drinking a Diet Coke. Being a former professor—probably at the Library of Alexandria—she made it a point to lecture me about my choice of beverage. With one hand on a cigarette, and the other pointing at my Coke, she explained how there were more chemicals in my drink than in her cigarette.

"I never drink Coke or any of those soft drinks. And, I never eat a hamburger. Those things will kill you," she exclaimed.

"What about cigarettes?" I asked her again.

"There are far more chemicals in Coke and hamburgers than there are in cigarettes."

I didn't argue. She can have her cigarettes, organic vegetables, and dreams of the Stalin Revival Tour. I'm sticking to my hamburgers, Cokes and the American Dream.

And besides, it's just bad form to debate food with someone who was a waitress at the Last Supper.

27

Making Memories

Every one of our *Travel Unscripted* adventures starts out the same way. We pile into a van or sport utility vehicle and head to the airport. At that moment I'm feeling a ton of energy, as I get excited about the adventure we are about to take. On the other hand, the crew is their usual stoic selves.

I usually find myself chatting up the driver while Nick and Gene each slip into a "road coma," There will be plenty of time to come up with our shots once we get to our location. For now, these guys are going to take advantage of any downtime. If you need an idea of what it's like to travel with these two, simply picture a guy who can fall asleep standing up. This is especially true of Nick. He has no problem catching zzzz's anytime, anyplace.

It's at these moments when I decide to pull out my iPhone and shoot some embarrassing video or pictures. I hope to capture a tongue hanging out or some drool running down the chin, if at all possible. Most of the time I don't get so lucky, but it's not for lack of trying.

I've been able to catch both guys in compromising positions, but prefer a segment I shot on our way to catch a flight to Tokyo. What's special about this particular clip is the timing. It was the middle of the afternoon and we were about fifteen minutes from the office when I asked Nick a question and didn't get a response. I looked over my shoulder and saw his head hanging with his chin just off his chest. As the SUV moved his head shifted slightly, not disturbing his peaceful sleep.

Nick was behind the driver and easy to see, but I couldn't see Gene because he was directly behind me. I quickly unbuckled my seat belt and swung around to get in a position to capture both of them on camera. I was going for the "buy one, get one free" deal. It didn't quite work out that way. As the camera landed on Gene it was clear he was awake and convinced yet again that I'm a fourteen-year-old boy in a man's body. His head moved from side with a look of disgust. He must have been thinking "It's already starting...Jesus!" Yes, my shenanigans started early on

Gene shows his disgust at my antics.

Payback is a bitch.

this trip as I was completely jacked up with unbridled energy. Hey, what do you want from me? I simply can't help myself.

When you travel unscripted, you run into a few surprises here and there. Sometimes it's a random person that leads you to a new adventure. Other times it's a byproduct of poor planning or bad luck. Most of the time the surprises come down to a random time and place where, given some prompting or cajoling, I find myself doing something that might be a bit out of character. Baby duck anyone?

I enjoy making these memories and sharing them with you, even when some of them might turn your stomach a bit! It's not like I tried to do that. It was all about the peer pressure at the time. That's right, I succumbed to peer pressure, or put another way, general pressure to do something fun for the camera.

Nick decides to give Sazae shellfish a try. Yum!

There are times when I just ham it up for some of the locals or tourists who are watching us capture a moment. At other times we stumble across a food stand and see something that goes beyond interesting. It's these moments where it pays to be the guy behind the camera, not in front of it.

Which leads me, once again, back to my crew. They have no problem in trying to convince me why I should try something weird or disgusting or just plain different for the camera. It's probably because they don't have to deal with the after-effects of some funky meal that might keep them up for a few hours that night. Whatever the reason, let's just say they have no qualms over making suggestions that they themselves wouldn't act on.

That changed one day in Japan when I tried something known as Sazae shellfish in a Japanese town called Matsushima. An old lady in a shop window was grilling up a variety of fresh fish and shells over an open flame. Being opportunistic we stopped and decided to shoot the experience. It's one of the few things I've eaten that I can tell you I will never eat again.

It's also the closest I've ever come to throwing up on the street. That's how bad it was. If you want the full sensation you'll have to imagine a thin sweat sock that's been worn for an entire season, without washing. The last game ends and the guy coming off the field hands you the paper thin sock with a little extra surprise. It's not bad enough that it smells awful and is damp with sweat. He's taken the added step of filling it with dog excrement. Now you are getting the picture, but you're not quite there. Throw it on the grill for a few minutes to get it heated up and voilà, it's ready! That's the best way to describe what I had just eaten on this street.

As I tried to wash the taste from my mouth while doing my best not to hurl, I was listening to Nick tell Gene how it couldn't be that bad. I gathered myself and suggested he give it a try. He continued to insist on how it wasn't bad and he'd have no problem doing it. "Go for it buddy" is all I could say. Misery loves company and I was looking for a comrade in arms.

I had a crazy grin on my face as I stood by and waited for the moment to happen. Don't be fooled by his expression or even his comments in the short video that accompanies this section. The worst part is the aftertaste and he was doing his best to play it down.

A full twenty-four hours later he finally admitted that he could still taste it in his mouth and that it was truly disgusting. I agreed. No amount of flossing, brushing or gum chewing could overcome the unique taste that one small creature delivered to our mouths.

This all comes with a caveat, of course. I'll take the occasional disgusting experience in exchange for all of the amazing things I get to do for a living. Indeed, I get to do what most people dream about and even get paid for it in the process. In a word, travel. And what's the best way to do it? Well, unscripted, of course!

Index

P

R

S

W

X

Y

Z